EDUCATION IN
A CHANGING WORLD

EDUCATION IN
A CHANGING WORLD

BY
EDWARD SHORT

PITMAN PUBLISHING

First Published 1971

SIR ISAAC PITMAN AND SONS LTD.
Pitman House, Parker Street, Kingsway, London, W.C.2
P.O. Box 6038, Portal Street, Nairobi, Kenya

SIR ISAAC PITMAN (AUST.) PTY. LTD.
Pitman House, Bouverie Street, Carlton, Victoria 3053, Australia

PITMAN PUBLISHING COMPANY S.A. LTD.
P.O. Box 11231, Johannesburg, S. Africa

PITMAN PUBLISHING CORPORATION
6 East 43rd Street, New York, N.Y. 10017, U.S.A.

SIR ISAAC PITMAN (CANADA) LTD.
495 Wellington Street West, Toronto 135, Canada

THE COPP CLARK PUBLISHING COMPANY
517 Wellington Street West, Toronto 135, Canada

© Edward Short 1971

0026960.
ISBN: 0 273 36117 1

370
SHO

Printed in Great Britain by
Alden & Mowbray Ltd
at the Alden Press, Oxford
G1—(G. 4652:15)

65499

Change is the nursery
Of music, joy, life and eternity

John Donne, *Change*

Contents

I

The Dilemma in Objectives

Education is about the way in which human beings live their lives. Its function is to improve the quality of life. But there are two views of human life, both valid and both the concern of the teacher. John Donne's oft-quoted assertion that 'No man is an Iland intire unto itselfe' (Devotions XVII) is a central part of the Christian ethic. But Bloody Mary in *South Pacific* was also right. We live our lives on the separate islands of our own consciousness with our own special hopes, experiences, loves, hates and dreams as the only other inmates.

No man can ever scale the cliffs of another's island. They are impenetrable except for the ability to communicate with other islands but the isolation diminishes as this ability improves.

It is not only the loneliness of the separate island which evokes and improves communication but also the certain knowledge that it is occupied only for a season. The loneliness and the transitoriness of man impels him to reach out to his fellows for companionship and security. The urge to do so is the oldest and deepest social need, and so he becomes part of a community bound together by a criss-cross of relationships. His isolation and insecurity are cut down to size. He is a separate island but, because of the limitations of his humanity, his island can never be quite 'intire unto itselfe.' The task of education is to enable him to live on his own separate island but also to live with others. It is concerned with the individual and with society.

Every baby born into the world possesses a potential for growth—to become a unique person as a result of all the experiences he encounters from the moment of birth, and there is evidence that pre-natal influences also affect his development. There is immanent in him a person of body, intellect, emotion and spirit. Education, i.e. the growth of this person, is not confined to school; it is continuous in every waking hour of life. Every influence leaves its mark however small. Formal education provides a specialised context for growth, for the unfolding of potential, for experience. Unfortunately, sometimes it is a context which is not conducive to growth. The world is full of 'mute inglorious Miltons' who never had a chance because of stunted educational objectives or unjust educational systems. How much neurosis in adult life is due to unease, often unconscious, about unrealised potential?

It is surely part of the social contract implicit in communal life that every individual should be given the opportunity to become truly himself, develop all his talents, find his true identity. After a century of state education we still fall far short of this happy state of affairs. Of course it is no easy objective for the educator and it is he who must bear the main responsibility for achieving it. Nor is it without risk for society itself. The individual who has found his identity may disrupt his class, his campus or his factory. On the other hand he may raise the whole quality of it by contributing his uniqueness to it. He may turn out to be a Hitler or an Albert Schweitzer. A major purpose of this book is to show that it is a risk we cannot afford not to take.

The constraints of communal life which never cease to multiply are only tolerable and justifiable if this risk is taken and the right to develop one's uniqueness conceded to all and not merely to a fortunate élite. This is the central, age-old dilemma of education. Individual growth demands freedom, uninhibited spontaneity and creativity but society demands conformity from its members. The problem is to reconcile freedom and conformity. The individual, unless he is a hermit living in a cave, lives among people and can never isolate himself from them. He must find a satisfying design for living in his relationships with family, friends, colleagues at work, etc., and these relationships demand both give and take. Inevitably they place limits on his right to do as he pleases.

'Shades of the prison-house begin to close
Upon the growing boy.'
(Wordsworth, *Intimations of Immortality*.)

as he learns the limits, learns to conform to society's ways and accept its values.

Society has traditionally looked to its educators and the educational institutions it has provided to conserve, enrich and transmit to succeeding generations the accumulated knowledge, skills, beliefs, values and graces on which its cohesion and permanence depend. Education is the keeper of a society's identity—a conservative function demanding conformity. At the same time it has the task of enabling the individual to find his—a function to which conformity is death.

The uniqueness, the originality, the newness, the creativity of the child, '. . . trailing clouds of glory' (*ibid.*) has to be reconciled in educational philosophy with the old and the orthodox. Finding a solution to the dilemma is doubly difficult because the physical matrix of the newness of the child, the human body and human nature, come from a distant Eden. 'Very old are we men' (de la Mare, *All That's Past*) and, like the society which nurtures us, we have accumulated deep-seated behavioural patterns. The quest for the holy grail of uniqueness has thus to use as its motive power an ancient, but extremely powerful, set of inherited drives which, undiverted, inevitably go their ancient ways. At the same time the questing must lie through the morass of societal values and taboos. The chances of success are, to say the least, not very propitious for a great many children.

From the earliest primitive tribes the community has been concerned in varying degrees with initiating its young into the requirements of adult life, sometimes by training, sometimes by precept, the process not infrequently containing an element of ritual. The objective veered between the two horns of the dilemma, more often than not towards the needs of society for conformity and competence in the necessary skills, less frequently towards those of the individual but rarely has there been a balance between the two—much less an attempt to synthesise them. Too often the need of the child to achieve his own perfection has been submerged in the attempt to 'fit him for life,' to make him a perfect little man who could drop competently into the adult slot, instead of a perfect child. At other times educators have refused to accept any social purpose whatever—an attitude not entirely unknown today.

Among the most primitive tribes, apart from learning the skills of survival, education was, and still is, almost entirely a preparation for the age-old customs and traditions of tribal life—

'Iron-jointed, supple-sinew'd, they shall drive and they shall run
Catch the wild goat by the hair, and hurl their lances in the sun;
Whistle back the parrot's call, and leap the rainbows of the brooks,
Not with blinded eyesight poring over miserable books.'

(Lord Tennyson, *Locksley Hall*)

The individual was not expected to deviate from the pattern and his upbringing had to mould him into it. He had no individual contribution to make apart from his share in the corporate task of preserving the *status quo*. There was no appeal to conscience and little to intellect. It was an almost mechanical conditioning, often ritualised, frequently on the level of the emotions—the dance and the tribal chant playing their parts. The individual was of no importance; the tribe was all important. This primitive concept of education is still a discernible strand in the philosophies of some late twentieth-century educators.

Jewish education in biblical times both in the home and the synagogue consisted of instruction in the Mosaic Law which, with its vast multiplicity of rules, governed both man's relations with God and almost every aspect of communal life. It differed from the practice of more primitive tribes because it was not only concerned with the transmission of a common pattern of life but also with the moral and spiritual good of the individual. The Jew had two allegiances, a social responsibility to preserve the fabric of his society intact but also a lonely, individual obligation to God. This was an improvement on the single allegiance of primitive man. Thus the ancient dichotomy of educational objectives began to emerge in embryonic form and were tolerably reconciled so long as the good which the individual was required to seek was the good acceptable to his society. There was no place for the pursuit of strange gods or the exploration of unknown paths. The individual could only roam between the high walls of accepted tolerances in behaviour and belief. Nevertheless, the tension between freedom and conformity was already potentially there as a result of the conflict of allegiances—a tension which was only too apparent when the young Jew of Nazareth refused to walk between the high walls. Indeed the clash of allegiances probably reached its greatest intensity in the early Christian Church. Absolute allegiance to Christ by the individual was an almost impossibly hard road to tread through rigid Jewish society and the barbarous Roman Empire.

In Sparta education had been primarily concerned with the wellbeing of the state but in the more liberal régime of Athens there was a recognition that the individual had an obligation to make his own distinctive contribution to the enrichment as well as to the permanence of community life. The assertion of individual responsibility was carried further by Socrates with his insistence on the right to question. Plato saw the problem of reconciling this right with the need to preserve a close-knit social order and his Republic was an attempt to reconcile the two. Free growth and spontaneity were to be permitted to his Guardians, but only along socially acceptable paths. The individual should certainly search for Truth but the direction in which he looked should be determined by the State's view of Truth. And there was no absolute concept of Truth; it was what the State said it was.

In medieval English society the feudal system allocated to every person his place from cradle to grave. Vertical movement in the social order was almost impossible. Education was a preparation for one's place in life. The Gild was the popular form of association serving social, charitable and educational purposes as well as its major industrial training and regulatory function. It was invariably based upon religious ideals and moral principles. Its educational function relied on apprenticeship but it was a good deal more than vocational. The apprentice was expected to acquire moral standards and a sense of obligation to his fellows as well as the skills of his craft and contentment with his lot.

There was no clash of loyalties as in the early Christian church. The individual's allegiance to God was expressed in the communal service of the Gild to the poor and the sick and this had the approbation of feudal society. Thus education was a synthesis of vocational, social and religious objectives. But, of course, as in Plato's *Republic*, freedom was 'cabin'd, cribb'd, confin'd' by feudal ideals and tensions. There was no place for the rebel in medieval society.

The university was much the same idea as the Gild, giving vocational training in theology, medicine and the law, but in a context of religion. Here also was a recognition that education is about the cohesion and permanence of society but also about the need of the individual to save his own soul.

Similarly, training for the orders of chivalry was also vocational but aimed as much at the stability of society as at the production of efficient knights, squires and pages. Training in manners, morals and religion were also an integral part of it.

From primitive society to the end of the medieval era the upbringing of the young had been overwhelmingly concerned with social permanence, with the training of people who knew the skills of adult life and also their place in the scheme of things. The only other allegiance ever permitted was that of the individual to God.

In the late fifteenth and sixteenth centuries the ancient, rigid pattern of feudal society began to change rapidly. With the Renaissance, man, individual man, in all his glory, came into his own. Educational ideas reflected the change in society and vocational and social objectives were relegated to second place by the pursuit of individual perfection. There emerged the idea of a liberal education concerned with calling forth (e = out + *ducere* = to lead) all the splendours of man, physical, social, moral, intellectual, spiritual.

'What a piece of work is a man! How noble in reason! how infinite in faculty! in form, in moving, how express and admirable! in action how like an angel! in apprehension how like a god! the beauty of the world!'

(Shakespeare, *Hamlet*.)

In the centuries which followed, the Renaissance ideal of educating the whole man persisted but became, in effect, the vocational training of the ruling classes. It created an ideal and socially acceptable type of man who was trained in the vocation to rule. Thus its purpose had swung once more from individual growth to social stability.

But the gradual use of the liberal ideal to serve vocational and social ends was not the only change which clouded the Renaissance concept. Hegel had the most profound influence on educational philosophy. He saw the state as a supra-personal entity with a life of its own. The individual had no reality or meaning apart from it. Hegel's ideas ran like an ominous strand through the tapestry of European history to the Great War and the inter-war dictatorships.

His influence on education in the totalitarian states through such educators as Giovanni Gentile was complete. Their systems were based upon the view that the individual person existed only to serve the state. He was a means to an end but not an end in himself. They challenged the assumptions about the individual and society on which educational practice had been based since the Renaissance. They also diverged from the liberal ideal in their use of propaganda, i.e. in the attention they paid to the unconscious part of the mind.

Hegel's influence on western education generally was to throw into high relief the ancient dilemma of the educator. Education is about the individual person but it is also about the society in which he lives. Theories about the relationship of man to society are the material from which educational theories are constructed. Hegel's theory of state absolutism was now elevated side by side with the Renaissance ideal of *l'uomo universale* and education became aware as never before of the struggle between the two.

His influence was seen in England in the public schools which

B

became more concerned with transmitting a code, with conformity and the preservation of the nineteenth-century class structure than they were with the liberal ideal.

However, some of the schools established after the Education Act, 1870, were nearer to Hobbes than to Hegel. In addition, they owed much to Victorian individualism. They recognised the individual and his right to question and enquire, to assemble his own data about a given problem and arrive at his own conclusions. The cult of individuality, for such it became in a limited number of schools, reached its height between the two world wars—perhaps as a reaction against authoritarianism. Its high priest was Sir Percy Nunn whose educational theories were based on the view that individuality is the ideal of life '. . . freedom for each to conduct life's adventure in his own way and to make the best he can of it is the one universal ideal sanctioned by nature and approved by reason.' (*Education: Its Data and First Principles*, Edward Arnold & Co., 1920.)

This rediscovered Renaissance ideal avoided vocationalism like the plague, indeed to such an extent that, where it held sway, education lived in an ivory tower far above the workaday world.

Nevertheless, throughout this century there have been increasing doubts about the wisdom, and indeed the morality, of an education pre-occupied with transmitting beliefs, values and standards to succeeding generations—and even about our right to do so—e.g., in recent years there has been a clamant campaign to end religious education in schools—children are not to be indoctrinated. But, at the same time, educationists such as Professor W. R. Niblett have increasingly re-emphasised the social purpose of education, the fact that a child must learn the ways of his society if he is to live happily in it.

Above all, perhaps, there is a greater awareness that there can be no individuality apart from society, that education, whatever else it may be, is a social process, that the child is what he is not only because of his genes but also because of the social context in which he lives and that his potential can only be realised in terms of his environment and his society and his experience of them.

Looking back over the changes of emphasis in education between the demands of society and the needs of the individual one is forced to the conclusion that in recent years we have come nearer to a synthesis of the need of the individual to become fully himself and the need of his society to perpetuate itself. Our teachers are now beginning to weave freedom and conformity into a reasonably coherent philosophy. A visit to a modern progressive primary school will illustrate the extent to which this is being done. It is not without significance that the National Union of Students in 1969 made voluntary communal service one of its major activities.

Of course, the apparent success of some schools in facing the ancient educational dilemma has been made easier by the abandonment of the myth of the stable society—

'Throughout our society we're experiencing the actual or threatened dissolution of stable organisations and institutions, anchors for personal identity and systems of values. Most important, the stable state itself has become less real.' (Donald Schon, *Reith Lecture*, 1970.)

In some ways it is easier to prepare children for an unstable society which they themselves can aspire to change.

Every new member coming into a group changes the group. Every child from the moment of his first conscious relations with his mother is making his impact on society. One child may grow up to walk 'beside the springs of Dove'; another to be a Napoleon, a Luther or a Ché Guevara. But whether he lives his life in rural obscurity or as a leader of men he will leave his mark on the groups in which he lives by deviating from conformity. There is unceasing change and renewal, sometimes ripples on the surface, sometimes a tidal wave of revolution which sweeps all before it.

The acceptance of instability today is however due to more recent and more turbulent factors, e.g. technological change which is transforming our material lives, greatly improved communications in every sense of the word, declining religious beliefs, changed attitudes to morality with their influence on sex, marriage and the family. Society has probably changed more in the past three decades than it did in the previous three centuries. It is this continuing and profound change in the inter-related complex of groups in which we live our lives that has made it possible for education to reconcile its quest for both freedom and social responsibility.

But a real doubt now arises. Is the basis of the reconciliation valid? Does it amount to anything more than swimming with the tide?— to participating in the socialisation of the child but only because of the throw-away nature of his social garments of belief, knowledge, manners, values, etc.?

The social function of education has been to create social stability. In accepting the instability of society are we now approaching the opposite function of fomenting instability? The validity of the reconciliation which appears to be emerging depends upon our attitude to social change beyond mere acceptance that a great deal is quite inevitable anyhow and that it is better for children to be able to adapt to it than to throw up their hands in horror against it.

And what is the consensus among those who teach and those who organise our education system about the major social changes we are seeing around us, about changing attitudes to authority or about changes in the class structure or about the disillusion with democracy? And what reply do we give to those who ask of us how our changing society can provide the security human beings need above all else if they know little and care less about their inheritance from it—in particular, about the firm anchors of transmitted values and beliefs which gave certainty, security and comfort to our fathers before us?

On the other hand, with the rapid growth of affluence, the more equitable distribution of wealth, the improvement in the living environment, social security, medical advancement, etc., is anything beyond the basic skills of civilised living and narrow professional competence relevant to the world in which our children will live and the challenges they will face? Do we need a God when technology can create a heaven on earth? Is the incentive of jam in the hereafter necessary when every Trade Unionist knows he can get jam today?

Questions of this kind about values and beliefs must concern all who are involved in education but there are even more doubts about other less fundamental aspects of the child's social education, e.g. to what extent should we insist on conformity to traditionally accepted patterns of behaviour? Must the boy be taught to give up his seat in the bus, to say 'Thank-you' or 'Good morning,' to wear trousers, etc? This last was the irreducible minimum of conformity but, after the revue *Oh, Calcutta!* does even that matter?

Education, its organisation, method and content, can never be isolated from social change. The Vice-Chancellor or the primary school teacher who sits in an ivory tower serves no one except, doubtfully, himself. It must be robustly responsive to the winds of change but not over-sensitive to every fashionable breeze.

But there is a resistance to change, a delay in response beyond mere inertia, described by Dr. Schon in his Reith Lecture: 'Organisations are dynamically conservative. That is to say they fight like mad to remain the same.' This is understandable enough in the schools and colleges in the light of their traditional function to preserve the myth, now seen as such, of social stability. Traditions of this antiquity die hard.

Provided that the response is not related to mere change of fashion but to major societal change, what should be its purpose: to oppose? to swim with the tide? to accelerate? to divert in another direction? To suggest that formal education can effect major social change in a society such as ours where it is one among many potent educational influences is to get its function and its effectiveness out of perspective. Formal education is only one factor among many in the upbringing of a child. In every moment of his life he is being educated, growing in response to his experience of the world of things, persons, ideas and feelings. Many experiences out of school where he is usually freer to follow his own passionate interests may be more intensely and more lastingly educative than his five or six hours a day for 200 days a year in school, e.g. school holidays for many young children in particular are of far more educational value than time spent on some of the more arid school activities. Or, again, the teacher may label this word or that as 'bad' language but father may pepper his conversation with it and he is certainly a man to be followed! The professional educator should be aware of his own limitations as well as of his opportunities. He cannot change the world but he may improve it.

In one sense however education can profoundly affect social change. Those responsible for the layout of the education system and for allocating resources to it both locally and nationally can enlarge or restrict opportunity and so contribute in no small measure to, or retard, change in society. On the other hand ministers responsible for major educational reforms, notably Mr. W. E. Forster and Mr. R. A. Butler, have perhaps had exaggerated expectations of the effects of their policies.

But the Education Act of 1870 did lead to a nation-wide growth of elementary education. This in turn generated the demand for widespread provision of secondary education which ultimately led to the 1944 Act and the spectacular growth of higher education we have seen in recent years. The development of the common secondary school after the second world war, but more particularly after Circular 10/65, is now making itself felt in an increased demand for higher education. Many boys and girls who, a generation ago, would have left school at 14 or 15 years of age to enter an apprenticeship or a dead-end job, now stay on, into the sixth form, qualify for higher education and eventually enter one or other of the professions. The number of 'O' and 'A' level passes has doubled in the past decade.

This book however is not concerned with the social effects of public policy towards education. Its purpose is to discuss some of the major changes going on around us and the ways in which education can make a positive response to them which will contribute to the enrichment both of our society and of the lives of the individual persons whom it comprises.

2

The Technological Revolution

The greatly increased production of wealth which technology is creating will provide the resources for improved living standards and for improving the quality of life generally. Education, housing and health probably have a greater bearing on the quality of life than any other publicly provided service, but all demand vast resources including manpower. Education, unlike the other two, generates its own demand—the more provided, the more demanded. In addition, industry's demands on it are becoming increasingly sophisticated.

The annual cost is now approaching £60 per capita of the entire population and rising at a higher rate than the growth in the gross domestic product. While technology is adding to this growth in the spiralling demands of industry for better educated entrants, it will, by the wealth it produces, generate the resources needed to maintain the growth in educational expenditure. It will increase the demands on education, but also provide the means to enable them to be met. But its influence will be very much more far-reaching than this, for it is changing society, and when society changes education must change with it.

The most obvious change in the past two or three decades has been the transformation by technology of the material context of life. But technology is not a modern phenomenon. The application of discovery and invention to material use is as old as man himself. It has brought him from the primeval forest to the skyscraper block by giving him the power progressively to exploit and modify his environment. It '. . . discloses man's mode of dealing with nature' wrote Marx in *Das Kapital*. It ranges from the first stone axe to the moon rocket. Its growth down the millennia has run parallel with man's evolution, but the bowler-hatted commuter of 1970—cosmic disasters apart—is not the end of the line. The process of technological change goes on, but with quite dazzling speed, and with it man's evolution. The problem now is whether man can keep up with his own technology. The leisurely parallel growth of technology and human evolution of the past is now out of gear—

'While science and technology have been bringing about vast changes in our material existence at an ever increasing pace, we have failed to match them with appropriate social and educational change.' (Lord Todd in his Presidential Address to the British Association, 1970.)

The technological factor most conducive to change is probably the development of electric circuitry, which is changing profoundly the control, scope and development of industrial production, communications, the storage and availability of data as well as a great many of the devices on which we rely in our everyday living.

In the mechanical age of the past century the production line concept has reigned supreme—in education no less than industry. Every desirable human activity has been broken down into simple units—knowledge no less than making Ford cars. Each simple unit demands its narrow, rigid, specialism—the school 'subjects' as well as turning the same nut on an endless line of products. Mass production of cars, houses, graduates, chickens—standardisation and specialisation have been the central features of our lives. Virtually the only scope for human endeavour has been to become a better specialist, a better nut turner, dentist or chicken rearer, than the other man, and so it has been an age in which creativity has been stifled and replaced by cut-throat competition, competition to become a better specialist.

For two centuries we have exploited the machine, but we have scarcely begun to exploit the enormous potential of man. Business

educ helps tech, tech helps educ

executives as well as school children have been powered by the need to 'get on,' to be better products of their respective production lines. One showed his graphs and the other his 'O's' and 'A's'.

But tomorrow will be very different—indeed today is already different. The mechanical age is rapidly giving way to the electronic age, quite breath-taking in its potential for improving the material well-being of mankind, but also in the freedom it can bring to the human spirit, freedom from standardisation and narrow specialisms, freedom from the production-line concept, freedom to create, to be different, to get to the heart of things instead of turning nuts or learning 'subjects' on their periphery. Computerised control of production can mass-produce products of infinite diversity, limited only by human creativity. Industry will be able to be increasingly versatile and flexible to meet volatile demand.

A consequence of new control systems is that virtually no unskilled or semi-skilled labour will be needed in industry, and the chief ingredient of the 'skill' required will be creativity, originality, perceptiveness, with manual skill and neat packages of factual knowledge of less importance. The end of the mechanical production line must, for this reason, end the nineteenth-century, mass-production approach in education which is rapidly becoming not only irrelevant, but a brake on progress. The new technological age demands a new man in place of the stamped-out nut-turner—himself a production line product no less than the product which he spent his life producing.

This is a central challenge of the new age to the conservatism of education, which, too often is quite unaware of the fundamental nature of the change which is transforming the satisfaction of our material wants and continues to prepare young people for a world which is disappearing. But the increasing sophistication of industry is causing other changes which must have consequences for education.

The pattern of industrial units is undergoing a rapid rationalisation, and one which is gathering pace, as Marx prophesied it would. Amalgamations and take-overs are an everyday occurrence and, as a result, larger units are emerging. Whole industries are now largely concentrated in two or three units, e.g. the chemical industry, and the process of concentration is probably greater in the United Kingdom than in the U.S.A., Germany or Japan.

But this coalescing does not stop at national boundaries. Enormous multi-national units are coming into existence—their turn-over often dwarfing many national budgets: e.g. that of General Motors, the world's biggest firm, exceeds the annual budget of Japan. Of the hundred largest U.S. firms in 1967, 62 had production facilities in 6 or more countries, e.g. General Motors makes more cars and trucks outside the U.S.A. than inside; I.B.M., the sixth largest U.S. firm, has manufacturing plants in 14 countries; Standard Oil sells more Esso in Europe than in the U.S.A.; I.C.I. makes more than a third of its investment outside the United Kingdom and has announced that it is increasing this proportion.

These are the new imperialisms, the successors to the old nineteenth-century empires. They are vast new centres of economic power—exceeding that of a great many sovereign states, but unlike them, not confined to any geographical area of the globe—

'Without a framework of political control they could, almost literally, take over the world.' (Anthony Wedgwood Benn, *Fabian Tract 402.*)

In addition to the changing patterns of industrial organisation with the multi-national firm, and the multi-national ownership of shares, the pattern of world trade is becoming inextricably interwoven. Design, research and marketing may be on a global scale. Management skills may move from one continent to another like the colonial administrator of the nineteenth century. The world market has been welded into one indivisible whole by these developments as well as by the pattern of agreements and organisations to regulate it.

The electronic control of production within the factory and the rationalising of organisation—often on a world-wide basis—outside it is leading to greatly improved efficiency, to an enormously enhanced potential for the production of wealth. For a number of reasons there is also a much better distribution of it—though the inequities are still considerable. On the other hand management is more remote from the shop-floor worker, although the large, well-run firm will counteract this remoteness by employing modern management techniques and practices. Nevertheless, major decisions affecting the working conditions, or indeed the livelihood, of large groups of workers are taken by boards which are geographically extremely remote—maybe in another country or continent. The effect of this growing remoteness on democracy is discussed in Chapter 5.

It must have consequences for education, not only in the narrow sense of providing management education of a kind which will be appropriate to the problems created by the new imperialisms, but also in educating men and women who can create and operate the kind of industrial relations needed in them.

And, of course, because of its greater sophistication and its larger units, industry will be much more vulnerable than in the past to the organised power of the worker. It is quite certain that international trade unions will emerge over the next two decades. In 1970 the T.U.C. organised a conference to discuss the consequences for the trade union movement of the growth of multi-national companies. In March 1971 the first joint meeting of the International Metalworkers' Federation of World Auto Councils was held in London. This was an attempt by car workers to follow air crews in negotiating improvements on an international level. This development, together with the interlocking system of world trade and of much of industry, will further increase the vulnerability of industry. This calls for a rank and file trade union membership of deep involvement, and which is well informed and responsible. This is yet another challenge of tomorrow which education cannot meet by ignoring even the existence of trade unions—let alone such refinements as the type of member they will require when they organise internationally.

What, then, are the consequences of these breathtaking technological and industrial changes for education? First, there should be no doubt about the need for reciprocal educational change. Factories, offices, homes, transport, communication, towns, have all changed out of all recognition in recent years, but many schools and

Edve so changing sleeve.

class-rooms are largely unchanged from what they were thirty years ago—both in appearance and in the activity within them. Their pupils are being prepared for a world which will soon no longer exist. There is more than a grain of truth in the old joke, updated, about the two seven-year-olds, reading a magazine about the speed of moon rockets in a corner of the playground, saying when the bell rang: 'Let's go and read some more Janet and John.' Indeed, bearing in mind the development of the mass media, and the intensely interesting world in which we live, we have almost reached a point where some children could learn more by staying away from some schools!

The mechanical age demanded uniformity and conformity in order to exploit the machine. Variety, creativity, originality, could be a liability on the production line or where the production-line mentality held sway. Of course, not all mankind were employed on a production line but its central economic importance left an imprint on almost every human activity. It got into the blood-stream of our society. In the electronic age the machine can be exploited to a degree undreamt of by Henry Ford by greater use of human intelligence and creativity and less of repetitive skills. After two centuries of machine-induced inhibition the wondrous creature—man—comes into his own again. It is as though Constantinople had fallen again, a new Renaissance, a rediscovery of man the individual after the dark age of man the cog.

This demands the abandonment by education of the whole production-line ethos with its fragmented curricula, its authoritarian methods, its stultifying hierarchy of examinations, its narrow limited objectives. In fact it demands a return to something like the broader educational objectives of the Renaissance,—the desire to learn, the love of learning, knowing how to learn and where to find information, objectivity, judgment, compassion—but subject to will, a sense of the one-ness of knowledge, an inquiring mind, an understanding of the basic concepts of both science, mathematics and the humanities, an acute appreciation of beauty wherever found, a willingness to strike out for '. . . fresh woods and pastures new'—flexibility, the development of each individual's uniqueness.

Of course, specialisms will always be needed, even in the electronic age, but they will be narrower but more volatile, and erected on much broader foundations.

Few men and women will spend their working lives doing the same job. They must therefore have the capacity and the adaptability to retrain a number of times throughout life. The educated person of tomorrow must be able to control the rapid change which technology will bring. Man must be dominant—not the electric circuit in the machine. All this points to the need for a greatly increased period of education proper and, almost certainly, a very much shortened initial vocational training—though, because of the need to retrain, vocational training will be dispersed throughout working life. The present statutory period of school life in this country just misses, at the beginning and the end, two of the most formative periods in life—the precious years from 3 to 5 when the brain makes its maximum post-natal growth, and the turbulent mid-teens. One would hope to see in this decade the ten-year period stretched out at each end by the universal provision of nursery education and the raising of the leaving age to 18. It really is no use the economist telling us we cannot afford the diversion of resources this lengthening of school life would involve. If we are to enable man to keep up with his own technology and Britain to improve its living standards, we cannot afford not to find the resources. The more affluent members of our society have raised the leaving age to 18 for their children, irrespective of their ability, and so the issue is whether or not we are prepared to educate the less well off—or continue to half-educate them. Nor would it make any sense to inject larger vocational elements into the later years of a longer school life. To do so would be to misunderstand the needs of the age of technology for more education first and less training afterwards. To purchase a higher school leaving age at this cost would be self-defeating.

At the tertiary stage of education there may well be a case for the integration of education and vocational training—indeed there need be no dichotomy. But in the age we are entering with its need for better educated people, there can be no case for it at the secondary stage. The formative years up to the late teens must be used to educate young men and women who can meet the challenge of the age of technology—whose youthful resilience is carried forward into adult life and not ossified by over-early vocational specialisation. And over-early educational specialisation is equally inhibiting. The sixth-form curriculum which consists of little more than two, or perhaps three, subjects for two years is, regrettably, still common. Whatever the schools and universities may claim for this practice, they cannot claim any educational merit. It is a negation of education which reflects little credit on either the universities, whose demands give rise to it, or on the schools who succumb to their demands.

However, in fairness to the schools, one must also point to the growing non-academic sixth form—16–19-year-olds who stay at school simply in order to continue their education, and not to acquire higher education entry qualifications. This is one of the more significant educational developments of recent years and one which will inevitably lead to a demand for similar facilities at the tertiary stage. Tawney's call for secondary education for all of half a century ago is within sight of achievement. In the 1970's the call is for tertiary education for all—the non-academic as well as the academic—but we cannot wait 50 years for it.

Until the polytechnics appeared there was little sign of response to this call from any higher education institutions, but their willingness to innovate and respond sensitively to change in society may well lead to new attitudes throughout the entire sector—provided they do not hanker after a medieval concept of status. The C.A.Ts. of the 1950's were drawn into the gravitational field of the universities. One would hope that the polytechnics of the 1970's will have sufficient attraction to draw the universities into theirs.

But whatever institutional pattern may emerge from the vast expansion in tertiary education which must occur in the present decade, the courses they provide cannot continue to be aimed at narrow, professional competence alone—or, if they do, they will not be serving their generation. They must be broader based—the arts graduate knowing some of the basic concepts of science and the science graduate not, otherwise, illiterate. The polarisation of the two cultures has reached a point where it must be regarded in the same category as the 11 + or the independent education sector—as a major divisive influence in society, and one in which our educational system can take no pride.

Higher education institutions must surely begin to cater for the non-academic sixth-former who wishes to continue beyond his late teens, to meander a little longer in the fields of learning of his choice rather than gorge at the trough of a vocational specialism—

'An increasing number of young people will enter higher educational institutions to prepare themselves for life in a more general way and for employment for which their degree course may not, and perhaps should not, give them detailed or expert knowledge. The time has therefore come when a very high priority should be accorded to the development of new and flexible patterns of study to meet the needs of many 18 to 21 year olds for whom the present, largely specialist, patterns are unsuitable.' (Dr. F. S. Dainton, *1870 Commemorative Lecture*, H.M.S.O.)

Of course society will always need its skilled doctors, lawyers, technologists, musicians, etc., but the new age will require from the vast and increasing majority, not excellence in a specialist field, but the broad flexible pattern of study to which Dr. Dainton referred. In fact we are being forced by this demand for better educated people to re-learn the old educational truth discussed in Chapter 3—that *what* is learnt is much less important than *how* it is learnt, and this is true from the primary school to the university. The factual content of teaching will in many fields be quickly outdated by new knowledge, but the electronic storing of knowledge and ease of access to it have made the memorising of blocks of information, which, nevertheless, are rapidly diminishing proportions of the sum total of human knowledge, a quite uneconomic use of a student's time. Mastering access to it is a good deal more important than memorising. Apart from these two considerations, most of it has always sunk down irretrievably to the bottom of the fish-pond of memory anyhow.

On the other hand sound teaching methods can be conducive to the growth of those very qualities which will be most needed towards the end of the century when today's primary school child will be in early middle life. Beyond the basic skills, which in the modern world must include such skills as a second language, and typing, it does not matter much what a child or a student learns. The educative effect of the freely selected task of learning sufficient about electronics to assemble a television set will be considerably greater than an examination board selected task of working through a syllabus in electronics. Knowing exactly *where* to find information about Tudor dress will be far more valuable than memorising an outline of the Wars of the Roses. Making a model of the Globe Theatre will be remembered throughout life, but an essay on the Elizabethan theatre will be forgotten next year. A mock general election is better than a lesson on the British Constitution. A project on *Employment in our Town* could arouse interests and uncover sources of information which would not emerge in a dozen class lessons. The multi-media foundation courses of the Open University, because of the excellence of method of presentation, are awakening enthusiasm for learning which will carry students through the more difficult subsequent stages.

Method has come into its own again. But herein lie two dangers which became only too obvious in the late 1960's in the chorus of demands for greater attention to method in the colleges and departments of education. This gave rise to the Area Training Organisation Enquiry of 1969 and the James Enquiry of 1970. Behind it undoubtedly lay the, often unconscious, feeling that in the new age the factual content of education is less important than the methods it employs. The first danger is that the clamour may lead to a reversion to the practice of half a century ago of merely training craftsmen instead of teachers, and the second is that of the young teacher leaving college with a repertoire of teaching methods which he will use for the rest of his life. It cannot be over-emphasised that teaching methods are, basically, personal relations which cannot be learnt in college and which every teacher must work out for himself with the help of more experienced colleagues.

The first requirement of the successful teacher is that he himself should be a well educated person in the sense that he possesses the qualities mentioned earlier in this chapter. He should also possess and constantly develop and enrich an educational philosophy of his own. The teacher who has stopped thinking about the wider aspects of his job is moribund. He should be familiar with the latest knowledge on learning and teaching as well as about such themes as intelligence and assessment. Not least he should know a great deal about sociology and the latest techniques of sociometry. What makes his pupils tick in the groups in which they live is essential knowledge. It would be a sorry day for a generation of our children if the present justifiable concern about method led to the production of rigid, inflexible teacher-craftsmen who had learnt in college exactly how to teach every fragment of knowledge with which they were likely to be concerned in their professional careers. How illogical it would be if the colleges returned to the concept of the production line, at the very time when industry, and indeed society, is moving away from it.

This chapter has been a plea for a broader based education throughout all its stages, in order to enable society in the future to exploit man, with all his glories, as fully as the machine has been exploited in the past two centuries. There is one sector of society however which calls for more specific education. There is a T.U.C. affiliated membership in Britain of 8,875,000 (1969 T.U.C. Report). The Transport and General Workers Union has 1·6 million members. The major unions may possess funds of many millions. Their activities profoundly affect the working conditions and living standards of the vast majority of the working population. Leadership of a major trade union is certainly comparable in complexity, in the skill, judgment and expertise required with top management in a major industrial undertaking—indeed there are no industrial companies in Britain with a labour force as big as the membership of the larger trade unions. I.C.I. has 197,000 (U.K.) employees— far fewer than a number of trade unions. The National Union of Teachers has almost as many members as there are people employed by the National Coal Board or the Post Office.

There is a large and growing range of courses and qualifications including degree courses for management aimed at industry and

C

commerce, but few opportunities for trade union officers. There are at the moment 62 short courses throughout the country, mainly in the evenings, for shop stewards. In addition there is the venerable one-year course in Trade Union Studies at the London School of Economics and a new full-time one-year course at Enfield College of Technology for a diploma in Industrial Relations and Trade Union Studies. Some of the courses at the 8 long-term residential adult education colleges have a good deal of relevance to trade union education—particularly at Ruskin College, Oxford. Unbelievable as it may seem, this appears to be the extent of the education system's provision of trade union education. It is pre-occupied with one side of industry and almost completely neglects the other. There are courses for doctors, lawyers, teachers, dentists, engineers, veterinary surgeons, architects, town planners, business managers— why not for trade union officers?

The growing power and responsibility of organised labour and the development of large, often multi-national industrial firms, calls for a response from the whole education system, but for more specific provision of opportunities for education in trade unionism at the tertiary stage.

A result of the production-line era in the first century of state education, with its fragmentation of knowledge and intense fragment-specialisms has been the cat's cradle of examinations in which our young people find themselves enmeshed from a quite early age. They are a necessary consequence of a system which puts on competition the excessive premium which our society has done. Creativity, originality, nonconformity, innovation, were not in great demand. Knowing more and more about less and less was what the mechanical age demanded. And so, with Victorian thoroughness and self-confidence, we divided knowledge into water-tight boxes and within the boxes were sub-boxes and sub-sub-boxes—the whole neatly conforming to a plan called a syllabus. Before the child could move from one plan to another he had to jump over a hurdle— to test his familiarity with the sector of knowledge he was leaving.

While examinations were inevitable in an age which believed

that all physical problems were best soluble if they were divided up into small operations in which specialists could be trained, they have now attracted to themselves a ritualistic function. They are part of the initiation rites into adult life—differing only in content, but not in principle, from those of primitive tribes.

Like many other aspects of the educational scene, we have grown so accustomed to them that we have come almost to regard them as part of the natural order of things. After all, we are told, competition, the struggle for survival, has been inherent in man's evolution and is today sublimated into a thoroughly wholesome motivation of effort in both childhood and adult life. It is natural. And has not every society, from the dawn of history, required of its youth certain achievements, often ritualised, before being admitted to full, adult membership? Initiatory hurdles are also natural. The trouble is that education always tries to rationalise its conservatism—the time-lag before it responds to change. It is surely high time it stood back and took a long cool look at the examination structure it has created and which not only has ceased to serve any useful purpose but is a major obstacle to true education. We persist in testing memorised areas of fact in an age when electronic devices can memorise them and recall them for us infinitely more efficiently than the human brain can ever do. We glory in testing the capacity to perform educational circus tricks while our testing techniques leave un-glimpsed, let alone assessed, the real objectives of education. The traditional examination tests what it tests and nothing more.

Because employers, parents and higher education institutions set such great store by examinations they have come to determine the curriculum of the secondary schools, as the 11 + examination did with the primary schools even long after objective tests were employed. The syllabus will almost always be prepared by a remote university examination board, a notable exception being mode 3 of the C.S.E., and it is as far from a child-centred curriculum as it is possible to get—indeed it is not even teacher-centred. It is an imposed curriculum and, as such, is a disincentive to any education worth the name. One wonders how much longer we can continue to ignore all we have discovered in the past half-century about how children learn and how to teach; how much longer we shall persist in hanging mill-stones around the necks of our children.

Of course assessments are needed towards the end of the secondary stage and in the tertiary stage for vocational guidance and choice. We ought, surely, to work towards the use of a cumulative record which tells a great deal more than the ability to cram and disgorge information. Until this is achieved much could be done to broaden the scope of examinations so that instead of focusing on the ability to cram and disgorge they search out other qualities, e.g. the ability to find and assemble information from books used in the examination room would be a good deal more sensible than the present insistence on memory to supply all the data. After all, our age has the computer and we don't need to continue training children to do the tasks they do more efficiently any more than we need to train them to light the gas by rubbing two dry sticks together—or even to use the great technological advance of the tinder box. But we continue to do so. The teacher feeds in the data. The examinations board writes the programme and, in the examination room, Johnny is expected to 'click-click' and produce the answer. But the answer reveals nothing about qualities of character, of heart and soul—creativity and ingenuity, about the wider objectives which technology and society have placed before education.

If the electronic age which we are entering requires from education qualities which are different from those which were most useful in the past two centuries of machine exploitation, new techniques for assessing them must be developed, for the traditional examination, which is almost entirely concerned with assessing the absorption and understanding of knowledge, is clearly quite inadequate. It assesses the educational standards required in 1850 and is powerless to measure those which will be needed in the year 2000. Here is an educational activity where radical change is long overdue.

So far this chapter has discussed the effect of technological change on society and the consequent response which is required of education, but there is another sense in which technology ought to be transforming the activity which goes on in schools and colleges, i.e. in the systematic application of techniques, resources, equipment, experience and knowledge to the learning process. The task of educational technology—a graceless term—is to help the teacher to solve the practical educational problems being thrown up by the kind of change discussed in this book.

Foremost is the need to give individual attention to every member of the class, an unavoidable problem with the demise of the class-lesson and lecture, and one made all the more difficult by research into the deleterious effects of streaming. As a result of these two changes in method and school organisation a majority of teachers today find themselves with classes of mixed ability all progressing at different speeds. A simple division of the teacher's time among the groups, or individuals, would mean only a few minutes of individual attention per child or group in each hour. It is the task of educational technology to find a better solution which will often be based on the concept of programmed learning.

Whatever the solution it must involve a continuous educative interplay between teacher and pupil, the dialogue which programmed learning involves; e.g. the Open University's programmes demand a response by the student at the end of almost every page before he moves to the next. The University is also employing the computer-marked exercise but only because it would be physically impossible to cope with tutor marking of such large numbers. However, there is little doubt that programming in schools will come to use the computer to develop and deepen the degree of dialogue between the programmer and the pupil. Pupil involvement in the learning process will then have moved as far as it is possible to get from the often non-involvement of the typical class lesson.

Some of the intensively practical problems to which the educational technologist is finding solutions concern resources—locating them, selecting the most appropriate for a given theme, obtaining them and deploying them to the best possible advantage. Others involve designing equipment specifically for educational use and defining its place in the learning process. In view of our new knowledge about the influence of social factors on attainment, finding the best techniques, resources and equipment to meet

special needs such as compensatory education for cultural deprivation, the immigrant or the child who has for one reason or another
missed a good deal of time at school, is equally important.

Science and invention have developed a vast range of resources
and equipment in recent years. Similarly, educational, psychological
and sociological research has expanded our knowledge about the
learning process enormously. Educational technology has the task
of marrying the two. It is not an up-stage name for audio-visual
aids, which, without skill in their use and an understanding of their
place in an organised learning system, are of little use.

Nor is it a Machiavellian government plot to replace teachers by
machines as was generally believed in the early days of audio-
visual teaching aids. Clearly some parts of the teaching process are
mechanical and repetitive and are done as well by a machine as by a
human being, but the human relationship between teacher and pupil
not only remains central to the learning process but will become a
great deal more important as the repetitive, memorising skills
recede in importance as educational objectives and the development
of individual uniqueness becomes our goal.

The teaching machine is complementary to the work of the
teacher—not a substitute for him. Far from reducing the need for
teachers, technology in the classroom is likely to create a need for
more and better trained teachers.

In the second half of the sixties teacher training capacity in
the United Kingdom was increased by 86 per cent with the result
that greatly increased numbers of newly-qualified teachers are
entering teaching in the early seventies. Many doubts have been
expressed about the extent to which the education service should
absorb its own product of highly educated manpower in this way,
but these tend to ignore the dual effect of technology in reducing the
demands of industry for manpower but, at the same time demanding
a greatly improved standard for its reduced intake. Thus, technological advance should make possible a continued diversion of men
and women into education, but it will also greatly increase its
demands on them.

The age of technology is throwing up its own terminology—

in education no less than elsewhere. We now have the terms 'curriculum development', which simply means the philosophy and content of education, and over-lapping it, 'educational technology,' which has the task of finding the most effective learning systems for achieving the objectives of curriculum development. The two terms have come to be associated with national bodies—the first with the Schools Council and the second with the National Foundation for Educational Technology, the Educational Foundation for Visual Aids and the National Committee for Audio-Visual Aids in Education—a triumvirate which is badly in need of rationalisation.

The two empires have been pushed out to include the whole educational process from the philosophy which inspires it to the evaluation of its methods. It is unfortunate that they should be clothed in new, and not particularly apt, terms. The result is that teachers are beginning to regard them as remote and rather technical disciplines on the periphery of the education service like psychiatry or sociology, which are the concern of enthusiastic experts outside the schools. Where this view is taken it is counter-productive to the efforts of the national bodies for the aim should surely be to convince every teacher that both curriculum development and educational technology are his job—his unavoidable job if he wishes to be a successful teacher.

However one highly desirable result of the empire building of educational technology has been its insistence on drawing together the whole learning process into one system—definition of objectives, selection of the appropriate media resources and methods to achieve them, implementation and constant evaluation. So often the new piece of equipment collects dust in the cupboard and is only used, almost on the spur of the moment, to reinforce methods to which it is not really relevant.

In recent years industry has produced a flood of new materials, resources and equipment which, when used intelligently, are transforming the learning process. But too often the technological revolution has not reached the classroom. The parsimony of some local educational authorities may be one reason for this, the inadequate dissemination of information and advice by in-service training or otherwise may be another, but a major cause is the reluctance of some teachers to abandon so-called 'tried and tested' traditional methods in the way that the industrialist, or even the housewife has done in recent years. Technology is changing the face of industry, the home, transport, shops, offices, entertainment, etc., but has not so far made the same impact on education. Yet the objectives of the electronic age with their emphasis on individual creativity cannot be achieved in the traditional teaching situation. Production line education must give way to systems which induce each individual to move as quickly and as far as his potential permits, but until a distant millennium when each teacher teaches one child this can be done only by the systematic use of equipment and resources which are planned, produced and deployed for the purpose.

Most young people today live in modern homes filled with up-to-date appliances; the motor-car makes the family mobile as never before and by the end of the century it may well have been replaced by the family helicopter; the family shopping is done in the super-market with its ultra-efficiency, excellent packaging and sweet music; increased leisure and higher incomes have made holidays abroad, weekends in the country, and cultural activities common-place; the mass media brings the world—and other worlds—into every living room; the persuasion of the ad-man is everywhere. This is the world which the application of science and invention has created. If education is to draw its material from the world of the child's experience, and to be effective it must do so, this is the context to which it must look—a world which is being transformed by technology—not the world at the turn of the century as it so often does.

The war changed society

3

Authority

The next chapter discusses the change from heteronomy to autonomy
in morals and its consequences for moral and religious education.
Perhaps the most obvious and disturbing manifestation has been the
virtual breakdown of authority as we understood it in the past half
century. The use of rationality as the touchstone of behaviour was
always inherent in the renaissance ideal. After Kant it was deified
for he '. . . dispensed with the hypothesis of God to account for the
source of the moral law' (J. A. T. Robinson, *Honest to God*, SCM
Press Ltd., 1963). The process accelerated after the first world war
with its break in the old continuities of values, standards, manners,
economics, etc. In the 1920's, influenced by Moore's *Principia
Ethica* and released from the horrors of war and the constraints of
the Victorian era, although immersed in those of unemployment,
society revolted against the authority of a code of moral values as
never before. In the Jazz Age young people did the Charleston until
day-break, abandoned their sense of sin and forgot about moral
obligations. The failure to tackle the chronic unemployment
problem probably owed as much to this change in ideas on morality
as it did to economics. The only consensus was that there should be
universal tolerance and that the old taboos should be discarded.
It was without doubt partly because of this change that the West
appeared quite incapable of withstanding the growth of the authoritarian regimes in Europe for the old standards which gave coherence

to a nation were crumbling. There was an authority gap, a crypto-anarchy, which was deplored but not understood. The desire to understand it and to put something in its place has not emerged until our own time.

The second world war severed what fragments remained of the docile stability of the late nineteenth century. The reaction to the excesses of the European dictatorship hastened the rejection of authority. The 'we want no Hitlers here' attitude has been used to justify many a revolt against management, don and government in the past twenty-five years. The reaction against authoritarianism added its weight to the rejection of authority and this was seen nowhere more clearly than in education. Progressive schools had for long been anti-authoritarian but the 20's and 30's saw the pursuit of individuality in education elevated far above the traditional educational objective of transmitting the values of society. The inter-war vogue of exaggerated individuality in the schools was undoubt-edly, in part, a reaction against authoritarianism which seemed to be gaining ground at an alarming pace and against which the western democracies appeared to be powerless and, indeed, to lack the will to oppose. It was as though education was determined to save the minds of men from fascism though democracy could not save their bodies.

Since the second world war the technological revolution has trans-formed the material context of our lives (see Chapter 2). One of its consequences has been as Marx predicted—the concentration of industry into larger units. This has enormously increased the power of labour to disrupt the economy and this enhanced power has emerged when both trade union and industrial leadership, like other forms of leadership, has been losing its authority. The result has been a vast increase in unofficial industrial action.

Before the welfare state the savage sanction of penury alone would have been a powerful deterrent but today, fortunately, no one starves and the power of organised labour is such that every striker, even the unofficial ones, can count on reinstatement. Today, the management—and often the trade union leader—have less authority than the shop steward.

It has also been the quarter century which has seen the end of illiteracy and the growth of the mass media which, with all its dangers, has given us a better-informed nation. People are no longer the 'dupes of crafty rogues' (St. Paul to Ephesus). They can't be 'taken in' so easily and 'taking in' was all too often an element in authority.

In Britain, as in some other European countries, we have the added factor of the psychological consequences of divesting ourselves of Empire. Before 1914 we had an assured role in the world. The morality of it worried few. Today, twenty-one years after Indian independence, there are signs that we are becoming reconciled to a new and more honourable role. The abandonment of an established national role which had become discredited in the eyes of the world and the quarter century of vacuum which followed have been nationally unsettling. When the power of the British Raj ended on the 26th January 1950 its power in Britain was not unaffected.

In the same period democracy has become more remote and unreal (see Chapter 5). It has never been applied to industry where decisions can have a more profound effect on men's lives than decisions in Parliament. Nor has it made much impact on the class structure of society with its hierarchy of wealth and privilege. Political democracy without social and industrial democracy has created disillusion with the authority of the state. Little wonder that the policeman is seen as the agent of an increasingly impotent and impersonal state.

Underlying all the political, technological and social trauma of the past half century has been the waning of religious belief. And, in the final analysis, authority depended upon the acceptance—willing or under duress—of a code of behaviour of the kind which the Christian ethic provided.

But an important aspect of the long tradition of Christian authority has been carried forward into modern anti-authority attitudes. Christ's authority depended upon a personal relationship and not on a command. As Professor M. V. C. Jeffreys has pointed out, there was no Christian authority without a free acceptance of it. (*Truth is not Neutral*, The Religious Education Press, 1969.) The authority and the human response to it were inseparable. The rebellious student today may accept the authority of the Senate of his university provided he is involved in its decision making. The authority of the university can only be derived from a freely accepted relationship with its members and not from its charter.

Similarly, the priest today cannot claim to wield authority by virtue only of his priesthood. It may be accorded to him as a fellow seeker after Truth. He will earn only derision if he tries to found it on any basis other than a free human response from his flock.

The breakdown of the old concept of authority and its replacement by authority flowing from a freely accepted human relationship is seen nowhere more clearly than in the home. The parent who demands respect because he is a parent will attract none. Consanguinity is today a quite inadequate basis for respect or the authority derived from it—even less for filial love. The quality of the relationship between parent and child will determine what authority the parent possesses. Again, as with Christ's authority, it cannot be based on command or injunction but only on free acceptance by the child.

Thus all the traditional wielders of authority in society—priest, parent, manager, policeman—are having to find new bases for their authority which are acceptable to the heirs of half a century of turmoil, war and change.

The teacher is not excluded. He has been affected probably more than any other and he has often contributed to his own problem by failing to synthesise the demands of the individual child with those of the society in which he is to live. Nor has he sufficiently criticised that society. Sir Alec Clegg at the Cambridge Union Teach-In on Education in October 1969 said 'There is a need for teachers to criticise the society for which their pupils are being prepared' (*Education for the Seventies*, Ed. Hugh Anderson *et al.*, Heinemann, 1970). However, whatever his share of responsibility for the disintegration of authority may be it is certain that he now bears a major part of the burden. It is equally true that neither education, the churches, industry nor the state have yet fully appreciated the nature of the change or adjusted to it. Disciplinary problems in schools, student protest, the fall in church membership, militancy in industry, mounting crime figures, low voting figures are all evidence of a change of attitude which is neither widely understood nor evoking a very positive response from those who ought to be concerned about it.

The response from education must involve its content and method as well as its organisation. The three are inseparable. First, however, it is important to consider the source of the teacher's authority. Professor G. H. Bantock has described the teacher as the necessary representative of authority because the child must '. . . learn respect for the idea of authority' and because the '. . . fact of authority enters into the pursuit of all knowledge' (G. H. Bantock, *Freedom and Authority in Education*, Faber & Faber, 1952). But this view does not make sense to the modern child. He will no more submit to the authority of the teacher merely because he is the teacher than he will to the parent merely because he is his parent. 'Do this,' 'Why?', 'Because *I* say so!' was always the formula of the ineffective teacher. Today it is a certain recipe for rebellion. The non-conforming child recognises no duty to submit to the teacher's authority as an agent of society nor to a school's imposed code of conduct. Of course he may be coerced into a posture of submission which masks the rebellious spirit behind it. If the teacher wants a quiet life, cares nothing for what lies behind the 'order' he has created or for his long-term influence on the child's life, a cane-up-the-sleeve attitude will serve him well enough.

Sanctions and punishment are utterly unacceptable today. The theory that they are a preparation for the harder knocks of adult life is demonstrably false and always was so. They are the certain road to an unsatisfactory adult life both as an individual person and as a member of a group—whether in family, office, factory or elsewhere. Artificial inducements are equally counter-productive. In the heyday of 11 + it was common form in middle-class families to offer the bribe of a new bicycle if Mary 'passed the scholarship.' One of the greatest problems of adult life is wrong motivation and it is often traceable straight back to a system of sanctions and inducements at school.

Can he base his claim to authority on his superior knowledge?
Before the second world war and the rapid growth of higher education, of technological change and the development of the mass
media which followed it the teacher was usually better educated
than the parents of his pupils. But the situation is very different
today, e.g. Britain has the highest proportion of qualified scientific
and technological manpower in the world at the 22–34 year age
group (source: O.E.C.D.). We are very nearly top in the percentage
of the population holding first degrees. Many parents are at least
as well educated as the teacher and, of course, children see and hear
an unending succession of Malcolm Muggeridges on television.
Teacher has lost his omniscience. He can no longer baffle his pupils
with science! No one stands in awe of his superior knowledge any
longer.

An older generation of teachers, and some younger ones, create a
spurious authority for themselves by trying to cultivate a 'forceful'
personality—a piercing eye and all that! How many of us remember
being told that we must dominate our class—stand well back and by
force of will and eye quell the unruly mob! But this differs little
from the cane-up-the-sleeve type of order. Both are authoritarian
and counter-productive.

This is not to say that the personality of the teacher is unimportant. It is, in fact, extremely important—indeed it is the key to that
complex of human relations in the school which, for want of a
better name, we call 'method.' This is a fact of which the vocal critics of teacher training lose sight. No one can ever really be taught
how to teach. He can learn the principles underlying teaching and
learning but as the methods he will employ consist of personal relations with his pupils he must work them out for himself by
practice. The most important element in the successful teacher's
personality is love for his pupils—love in the theological sense, the
committal of will to their well-being, and not in the pop-song sense.

Perhaps the greatest and most widespread fallacy of all about the
teacher's authority is the belief that there is a technique called
'keeping order' which can be taught by colleges of education
and acquired by the diligent student. But very often the kind of

order meant was not order at all. It was silent conformity to whatever the teacher decreed.

The principal ingredients of order in school are purpose and love.
They are also the only safeguards of freedom. 'The need of the
world now is not more liberty for the exercise of men's various
faculties, but some purpose in life which may give significance and
harmony to the enjoyment of that liberty' (William Temple).
The purposeful school or class will rarely be a silent one. Nothing
could be more unnatural than a silent child anchored to one desk
for long periods each day. Little wonder that many people are
repulsed by the very mention of school when their schooldays are
remembered as dreary wastes of ghostly silence and inactivity.
Children ought to be free to talk and walk about as their common
purpose demands.

It is at this point that the order of a school is inextricably intertwined with both the method and content of the teaching. Purpose
is one of the bases of order—but whose purpose? The teacher's or
the child's?

There is a very old truth about education which we have tended
to forget in the broiler conditions of recent years but which is once
more attracting attention. It is that *how* we teach is a good deal more
important than *what* we teach. The accumulation of knowledge is
now so great and is increasing so rapidly and electronic methods of
storage and access to information have been perfected to such an
extent that it is becoming less important to memorise vast chunks
of knowledge than it is to know where to find them. Much of the
content of teaching will quickly become out of date or be forgotten
but the effects of sound teaching methods will become part of
personality and endure for life.

A second consideration which has a bearing on the question of
'Whose purpose?' is that we are dealing with children and not
miniature adults. Childhood has its own perfection. Achieving it
should be the aim of every teacher. There cannot be a perfect frog
unless there is a perfect tadpole first. Now, of course, every child
must acquire the skills of civilised living, in particular, literacy and
numeracy—but he will do so for his own purposes if he is allowed to

work towards them (see Chapter 8). Beyond that, do we really know what is best for the child or the student? More often than not he is given a carefully worked out syllabus in each of a number of artificial boxes of knowledge called 'subjects' which his teacher thinks he ought to acquire in order to graduate into adult life. The criterion is not the needs of a child or student but the needs of an adult. We are trying to make frogs without tadpoles! Clearly, the notion that the teacher, the parent or the priest knows what is best for the child is pushed much too far in our society. The principal determinants of what a child truly learns are his own interests and his own experience.

These two factors—the primacy of method over content and the objective of childhood's own perfection—together point the answer to the question—whose purpose? The only worthwhile basis for school discipline is a child-derived purpose, understood by all, helped forward by a teacher posture which is neither fussy nor heavy-handed, is constantly helping and caring, does not apologise for itself but makes no pretence of omniscience either.

This kind of discipline based on free acceptance of an intensely relevant purpose and not on sanctions or patently silly inducements is the only possible basis for a tolerable community life in school in an age when in adult life the old constraints of poverty, unemployment and eternal damnation no longer deter. The old, externally imposed discipline engendered hypocrisy and falsehood because when the disciplinarian was removed, whether he was parent, teacher or policeman, there was no discipline. The child today will behave with care and concern for others only if *he* is convinced that it is right to do so and not because he has been conditioned, like a dog learning tricks, to act in a given way in a given set of circumstances.

The masterly inactivity of the teacher has been mentioned but what of the time-hallowed class lesson, and its counterpart the lecture, in higher education? Generations of teachers inspired by Herbart's teutonic thoroughness have taken great and justifiable pride in the imparting of knowledge—indeed they raised the class-lesson almost to an art form. Many present-day teachers will recollect

the notes of lessons, setting out the formal steps, they were required
to prepare as young teachers.

In an age which is past—or is it?—when John Locke's *tabula rasa*
theory dominated the schools and teaching consisted of imparting
knowledge and the teacher's authority was assured by the accepted
code of behaviour, the class-lesson was an appropriate technique
but today, as a regular class-room activity, it no longer serves the
ends we seek. No class, even in a school which is streamed by ability,
is so homogeneous in ability or attainment that it can be taught
efficiently in a single group. The teacher who attempts to do so will
probably aim at the mean. As a result some children will be lost off
while others will not be stretched to their capacity. The sub-division
of the class-unit into groups of five or six children is now becoming
the normal practice. The greater part of the child's school day is
spent in the security of the small group with occasional class
activities such as music and discussions.

The acquisition of knowledge, though still important, becomes,
paradoxically, less important as the sum total of knowledge increases
but mastery of the access to knowledge becomes much more
important. But our knowledge of how children learn has increased
enormously during the past quarter century. We know that facts
which children find for themselves in order to further a purpose
which has gripped their interest and imagination are memorised
and can be recalled better than facts emerging from the best prepared class-lesson on a subject chosen by the teacher as part of a
course of study.

The class lesson is inefficient but it is also unacceptable to the
modern child. It is essentially authoritarian. The truth is what the
teacher asserts and the child is required to accept it. It is based on a
vanished concept of pedagogical authority. The university lecture
is even more unacceptable, particularly to students who did not
have to endure an endless succession of oral lessons at school.
There are still far too many lecturers who enter the lecture theatre,
open their note-books, deliver their lectures, close their books and
walk out without any opportunity for discussion or dissent.
The thoroughly inefficient and unacceptable teaching methods

D

of many university lecturers are a major cause of student unrest. We surely have now reached the point where university teachers should be required to undergo some professional training. The work of Professor A. M. Ross, Professor of Educational Research at Lancaster University, among others in this field, shows great promise and should be more widely known.

The important fact is that no teacher from primary school to university can count on possessing the kind of authority which previous generations of teachers acquired as of right. Their authority today can exist only in the free response of those they teach and getting that response is a tremendously demanding process.

Content, method and discipline have been discussed as three aspects of the activity which goes on in a classroom. The framework for the activity, the organisation of the school, is equally affected by the breakdown in authority. Three aspects of organisation are particularly important, rule making, the basis of the school teaching unit and the position of the head teacher.

Every community requires some rules in order to ensure reasonable freedom for the individual. But if rules become too obtrusive and are made for their own sake they endanger and indeed restrict freedom. If the aim of law is to preserve the maximum amount of individual freedom compatible with community life there is a point beyond which the multiplication of laws becomes counter-productive. Educational communities whether schools, colleges or universities, are no exception. Their rule structure should be kept down to an irreducible minimum even if some risk of marginal chaos is involved.

A framework of rules serves another purpose in the case of younger children. It is the almost universal experience of primary school teachers that their children feel more secure in a sensible rule context. It is, of course, important that this primitive unthinking reliance on rules is not allowed to persist as the child grows older. He must learn to think for himself and apprehend the consequences of his actions.

But the rules, if they are to guide conduct, must be clothed with authority and this brings us back once more to the two requirements that their purpose must be understood by all and freely accepted as a worthwhile purpose by at least the majority. Without free acceptance they possess no intrinsic authority of their own. These two bases for the authority of the rules are much more likely to be present if the people who are expected to obey them are involved in making them.

'Student representation' and 'pupil power' are new and so far as the latter is concerned, rather silly, battle cries on the campus but the idea they embody is as old as the hills, e.g. at the beginning of the century Homer Lane established and ran with great success his Junior Commonwealth in Dorset. At first its pupils were teenage delinquents but later others were admitted. Both discipline and the government of the school were entirely in the hands of the boys and girls. The only authority was the code of conduct which they worked out for themselves. This school was based upon a similar project in the United States, the George Junior Republic.

It is difficult to see how the universities can cling to the concept of a self-governing body of scholars, which is the basis of their treasured autonomy, with the majority of the undergraduates unenfranchised. Authoritarian government of a university by a professorial oligarchy is a survival from the past which, not unnaturally, provokes acute resentment among present-day students. The day has gone when edicts could be handed down from the Senate like the Law from Sinai, pinned on the notice-board and, *ipso facto*, command the obedience and respect of all to whom they referred. Autonomous morality demands that students themselves have a hand in making the rules within which they are expected to live.

Similarly the wise school, while having as few rules as possible, will allow its pupils to make as many of them as possible and will consult with them and discuss the rest. A free society cannot be sustained by an authoritarian system of education. Perhaps the freedom of our society would possess more reality if our children were nurtured in freedom and given the chance to acquire the self-discipline which it requires in order to survive.

An increasing number of schools have established school, house or year councils. There is no reason why this kind of machinery should be confined to secondary schools. In a primary school with the right kind of personal relations it is equally possible to mobilise the public opinion of the pupils in guiding the life of the school.

Malcolm Ross, the headmaster of a large London comprehensive school, has written as follows of his school—

'Like all other schools, we have our little patches of curriculum labelled social studies, general studies, and the like. But like all other schools we give our children the feeling for society far more by the modes of our communal life than by any contrived programme of study. The challenge has been to create a complex of self-governing units, the tutor groups, who during every dinner break demonstrate their capacity to govern themselves, simply by taking responsibility for their own bases, the tutor rooms. . . . It is the job of the tutors to train their groups in attitudes of responsibility which are tested in the free use of rooms at midday. It is the job of the prefects to see that within the complex of our seventy tutor groups, the operation of different peer groups do not conflict unacceptably. . . . It is the job of those teachers who are willing to be deployed to collaborate with the prefect to act as mentors, moderators, and interpreters, in this combined operation.'

This example has been quoted because it lifts the whole question of the devolution of responsibility for an orderly school life on to a more hopeful level than is often the case.

The larger secondary units demand devolution—a wider sharing of authority—but, more important, the whole spirit of our society demands that authority should not affront the dignity of human beings—whether men and women or boys and girls. It will not do so if it involves the free acceptance of those over whom it is exerted. If it does not do so it degenerates into avid authoritarianism which our age rightly rejects.

Devolution involves the sharing of responsibility both between the head-teacher and the staff as well as between the staff and the pupils as opposed to its concentration in the hands of either head or staff. If it is not shared in both directions there will be no authority worth the name. The autocratic head whose every word was law has gone, or should have gone, from our schools. Today's head, whether of a village school or of a 2,000 strong comprehensive school, sits not at the apex of a pyramid of authority but at the centre of a network of human relations involving teachers, pupils, parents and non-teaching staff. It may well be an uncomfortable seat but it is one which is well worth occupying.

Another pressure for devolution of responsibility has been emerging for some time in the changing basis on which teachers are paid. Eric Robinson discussed this point in the Autumn 1970 issue of *Socialism and Education*. He pointed to current moves to extend to the schools the higher education system of payment according to function. The thinking of the local education associations is moving firmly in this direction and, in spite of the sensible defence of the basic scale concept by the teachers' organisations with its additions for responsibility, experience and qualifications, it seems inevitable that teachers' salaries will give much more weight to function in future.

The consequence of this must be that the higher salaried teacher will attract more authority and responsibility, not the rather spurious responsibility so often associated with graded posts but formal responsibility which previously was concentrated in the head teacher. As Mr. Robinson pointed out, the alternative to this formal transfer would be a quite unacceptable degree of patronage. Thus the trend involves a further limitation of the head teacher's authority.

A third element in school organisation where modern attitudes to authority are bringing pressure for change is the way in which teaching groups are formed—'streaming' or 'non-streaming.' Streaming is based upon the view, the quite mistaken view, that if the class is more homogeneous in ability it can be taught more effectively. This point of view is still put in all seriousness by teachers who have largely abandoned the class-lesson, organise their classes in small groups and talk of child-centred curriculum. Of course there can be no homogeneous group of children. Every child has a unique pattern of ability. Even in the streamed selective grammar school the range of ability is considerable.

The streamed class is, unlike the modern approach to discipline and curriculum, a device for the supposed convenience of the system. It is teacher-centred not child-centred. It begins as the teacher's assessment of the ability of his pupils but soon comes to represent his expectations of his children and inevitably ends up representing the children's expectations of themselves and as a consequence it determines their performance. The labels 'A,' 'B,' 'C,' etc., pinned on so many primary school children leave an indelible imprint on their attitudes, their educational attainments and their vocational opportunities. At the Cambridge Union Teach-In, already referred to, in October 1969 Professor Hilde Himmelweit described research which showed that the stream in which a child found himself at the age of 13 was a better prediction of his future employment prospects than either ability or social background. She concluded: 'I would say that we have in this country an educational system which is probably unique in the world in the sense that we groom for failure as assiduously as we groom for success. We do not intend to groom for failure. It is merely a by-product of the system we are operating.' (*Education for the Seventies*, Ed. Hugh Anderson *et al.*, Heinemann, 1970.)

Dr. J. W. B. Douglas in *All our Future* (Peter Davies, 1968) revealed the extent to which performance at the secondary stage is determined by streaming in the primary stage. Performance is depressed more by primary streaming than by either I.Q. or social background. This is a waste of ability which cannot be justified on educational, moral or economic grounds. But, perhaps even more unfortunate, is the effect of streaming on attitudes. Professor Himmelweit's results showed that no matter what the ability of children labelled 'C' might be they developed resistance to change and risk-taking and became excessively nonconformist. The reverse is true of children labelled 'A.' And these are the characteristics which will least fit children for the world in which they will live at the end of the century. Flexibility, adventurousness, willingness to face accelerating change will all be required of them. But, above all, they will have to possess confidence in themselves and courage to question authority if they are to retain their freedom in the face of technological advance. But only the 'A' stream are being equipped to meet this challenge. We are failing our children if we continue to devalue the majority and overvalue the minority as at present. The latest of a long but recent line of research reports which comes out firmly against streaming is that of the National Foundation for Educational Research (see Chapter 5). Nicholas Bagnall in the *Sunday Telegraph* described the report as 'illusion-shattering'—the illusion being the view that streaming helps the brighter pupil.

The evil of streaming is as great in the comprehensive school. With the ending of 11 + selection the classification within the common secondary school can take on to itself all the divisiveness of the selective system which the school has replaced.

The case against streaming has been made in passionate but telling terms by Albert Rowe in '*Where?*' Supplement 12, 1968, and in equally forceful terms by Bruce Kemble in *Looking Forward to the Seventies* Ed. by Peter Bander (Colin Smythe, 1968). In *Education for Democracy* (Penguin, 1970) Mr. Rowe says 'Our society needs intelligence and expertise, *but allied to a new democratic concern for others*. Not trained intellects alone but *feeling intellects*. . . . Of course we depend on the intellectuals, but equally we depend upon "the others," upon their skills and qualities as human beings also. This means that one has to take an optimistic, democratic view of all pupils, their nature and potentiality.'

The damning of children by label, for our own convenience, defeats the progressive efforts which are being made in other aspects of school life to fill the authority gap. It can only be filled by free, reason-based response but this depends upon the child's confidence in himself and in his ability to decide what is right and what is wrong. If the decision which the school makes about his ability is clearly unjust there is little chance that his decisions affecting his fellows in school, home or adult life will be reasonable or just. If we destroy his confidence in himself by labelling him as second-rate, i.e. 'B,' 'C,' etc., how can we expect him to believe that he is capable of making rational humane decisions? And if he lacks the confidence, and therefore the will, to make them for himself he will leave school extremely vulnerable to those, of whom there are always many, who are only too ready to make up other people's minds for them.

6 Education can make a major contribution to filling the authority gap but it cannot do so by precept alone—even mainly by precept. It has become a major educational objective but it is one which involves much more than the content of education. The headmaster who asserts at the morning assembly that lying is 'wrong' and expects it to disappear from his school from that moment will be sorely disappointed. His pupils must, by their own reason and feelings, be convinced that it is wrong and the school must be organised in a way which is not based on untruthful assumptions.

In the last analysis authority depends upon ideas of 'right' and 'wrong' and today these ideas are formed much more in the minds and hearts of individuals than in accepted codes. The task of education is to ensure that the minds and hearts are equipped by practice, by trial and error, by example, by environment, by care and affection, by the whole ethos of the school, to make decisions which will raise and not depress the quality of life in our society.

4

Religion and Morality

At the end of the second world war when the Butler Act was being drafted, it was assumed, though even then it can hardly have been true, that almost everyone, and particularly most teachers, were adherents of some branch of the Christian church, even if some of them, as a cynic remarked, merely liked to have a church to stay away from. This assumption can no longer be made although, as a recent sociological study by Martin has pointed out, it is possible to exaggerate the extent of our secularity (D. Martin, *A Sociology of English Religion*, S.C.M. Press, 1967).

It is certainly true that we have become increasingly a secular, multi-cultural society in which allegiance to Christian belief can by no means be taken for granted. Nor should this be regarded as wholly loss. Very often in the past all we achieved was a posture, a façade of faith with little reality behind it. Who knows what went on in the minds of children behind the angelic 'Eyes closed: hands together'?

Of course, no one can ever be made to believe anything he does not want to believe, and it is surely better that the unbeliever should freely admit that he is an unbeliever than to adopt the pretence of commitment. It is surely gain that people should feel free to throw off hypocrisy and to express publicly what they sincerely believe—or do not believe—provided, of course, that they respect the rights and consciences of others.

In the years 1964 to 1968 inclusive there was a net increase by

47

migration of 142,600 Asian Commonwealth citizens in Britain. This has brought difficulties for teachers engaged in religious education, but it can also bring positive advantages, not least in forcing us to remember that we are citizens of the modern shrinking world, that we share the 'human predicament' with people of many races and creeds, and that we must learn to work together if mankind is to survive the crises and reach the heights which our modern prophets, both religious, scientific and political, place before us. If religion means anything, it should surely be pre-eminent in providing common ground in which men of all faiths—or none—can meet, and although many pages of its past record do not seem very propitious in this respect, there are paradoxically real grounds for hope in the present situation.

But the decline in Christian commitment has not been the only change. At the same time, perhaps partly as a result of it, or an effect of it, there has been a great upsurge of radical theology—in its own way as fundamental as the Reformation. Modern man and the modern child are, in spite of their shortcomings, nothing if not honest. They refuse to be put off by obscure theological jargon, and there is no field of knowledge where, faced with a problem or lack of a definition, it is easier to regress into jargon.

Bonhoeffer wrote from his Nazi prison about 'religionless Christianity' and today Bill Smith of Acacia Avenue argues that he can lead a Christian life without having to accept the Virgin birth, walking on water, and turning water into wine.

Honest to God (J. A. T. Robinson, S.C.M. Press, 1964) exploded the bomb of the new theology on our own doorstep. Things would never be quite the same again.

Those involved in education could bury their heads in the Bible story narrative approach no longer. They were now faced both with a questioning of Christian belief as never before, radical and invigorating questioning by those who still wished to believe, and with forthright but honest rejection of it by others.

How could religious instruction have any coherence among these rapidly shifting sands of belief and commitment? Fortunately there have been many dedicated teachers, H.M.I.'s and Directors of

Education who have regarded these changes not with dismay or resignation but as a challenge to improve the whole approach to religious education. In particular more attention than ever before is being paid to moral education and its relationship to religious education. For a major consequence of the growth of secularity and the flood of radical theology has been an almost universal discarding of the view expressed by Mr. W. E. Forster in 1870 that morality can only be based upon religious belief '. . . but I think we all of us agree that the standard of right and wrong is based on religion and that when you go against religion you strike a blow against morality' (Hansard, 14 March, 1870 [Col. 1938]). Plainly such a view is untenable to a great many people. The humanist or the agnostic believes he can live a perfectly good life without Christian belief—and of course he is right—

'In a world which generally accepted the Christian view of life here and hereafter, the Clergy were able to propound the Christian faith in their own terms on their own ground. They can no longer do this in a plural society. The Christian message has to be translated into secular terms on secular ground, a process the more complex as that ground now changes so fast.' (From a letter to *The Times* from the Bishop of Horsham, 27 November 1970.)

Rational judgment, and not religious belief, determines, for most people, what is 'right' and what 'wrong,' although many would admit that Christianity offers the deepest moral insights—that there is in it '. . . a crystallization of man's moral knowledge and the use of this as a basis for understanding the nature of God in moral terms and man's relation to Him as a moral being' (Professor P. H. Hirst, *Let's teach them Right*, Pemberton Books, 1969).

The simple assumption which apparently lay behind many of the speeches on the passing of the 1944 Act that, to put it crudely, an extra dose of religious instruction was all that was needed to cure the moral ills of the nation is today seen to be invalid. Too many people have disproved it in practice by discarding the moral teaching they have received along with whatever they learnt at school of scripture. And many philosophers, such as Professor Hirst, have argued powerfully against it by upholding the autonomy of morality, a doctrine for which they can find some support in the Epistle to the Romans (Romans ii. 14–15). The gentile also knows the moral law—not from the Law of Moses but from nature.

The secularisation of society, the radical theology and autonomous morality are part of the contemporary scene which cannot be ignored. But what of standards of morality? There is a popular belief that we are going to the dogs—particularly the young.

Modern youth is, of course, radical, iconoclast but also idealist. He wishes to take the world and—

> '. . . shatter it to bits and then
> Remould it nearer to the Heart's Desire.'

He will no longer accept views simply because they are the views of his elders—indeed he will often reject them for that very reason. Nor will he accept authority imposed on him arbitrarily by school, priest, home, college or state. In all this he is not very different from the youth of all ages. He does, however, feel perhaps more intensely than we imagine about the gigantic imperfections in our society—the Bomb, the maldistribution of wealth, hunger and poverty. They are repugnant to his idealism. He is also often deeply involved in community service.

What then are we to make of him—with his long hair and outlandish clothes—this lovable, hatable, but quite unavoidable part of the current scene? Is he, indeed is society itself, going to the dogs, and, if so, how do we stop it?

Clearly, the starting point of the answer to this question is to be clear—if that is possible—about what 'morality' is. Everybody feels strongly about it, but few have anything but the vaguest and most prejudiced idea of what it means. As Harold Loukes has pointed out, there used to be a view that the moral code which determined what was 'right' and what was 'wrong' was established and maintained by our betters, '. . . some sort of élite: an aristocracy, maintained in sufficient comfort and elegance to enable them to have superior moral insight; a church, exploring revelation and developing superior moral insight; moral philosophers, speaking from an assurance of their intellectual superiority' (*Let's teach them right*, Pemberton Books, 1969).

Ordinary people may have diverged from it, but their consciences were salved by the knowledge that, in the class-structure of morality, somebody, somewhere could always be relied upon to keep the moral code afloat.

But today the idea of a code—providing for most people a groundwork of rules—has well nigh been replaced by the individual person using his own reason to decide what is 'right' and 'wrong.' Unfortunately, all too often, the touchstone is his emotions and not his reason. Traditional values find little acceptance except among those whose niche in society can only be preserved by defending them. The Victorian code of our fathers has become merely one of a number of options as a basis for behaviour.

Many factors have contributed to this change—Freudian psychology, modern psychiatric practice and the exaggerated cult of individuality in some schools among them. Perhaps the most potent of all has been the breakdown in authority—discussed in Chapter 3, for authority and a generally accepted code of morality were inter-dependent. Those in authority could safely make assumptions about values and therefore about reactions to their activities. This is no longer possible. With the decay of authority, leadership has lost its credibility and this applies to codes of behaviour as much as to anything else.

It is extremely difficult to find criteria to measure the effect on standards of the abandonment of a code and its replacement by individual decision. Crime figures have risen dramatically, but a vast area of 'crime' has little relevance to morality.

Persons found guilty of all offences in England and Wales
1968—1,576,868
1960—1,035,212
Persons found guilty of indictable offences in England and Wales
1968—257,327
1960—163,482

The divorce rate shows a similar increase, but there can be little morality in a marriage of utter incompatibility, which today is often ended, but in the past would have been maintained for the sake of appearances.

Decrees absolute granted in England and Wales
1969—50,063
1959—23,837

The increase in illegitimate births is clear indication that the old taboos about sex before marriage are no longer a deterrent.

Percentage of illegitimate births in England and Wales
1969—8·5
1959—5·1
(Source: Annual Abstract of Statistics No. 107, 1970.)

If we add to this apparent statistical evidence of disintegrating standards—or different standards—some of the more obvious manifestations of cynicism, lack of idealism, selfishness ('I'm all right Jack'), cruelty, etc., which we see around us, it appears to add up to a thoroughly unsatisfactory state of affairs—until we look at the other side of the coin. There can be little doubt that society is more compassionate in its concern for the sick, the elderly, children, mentally afflicted, prisoners, the poor, the underprivileged, under-developed nations, animals, etc. For example, the obscenity of hanging has been abolished in Britain. In the 'good old days' when life was guided by the moral code it was applied for the minor deviation of stealing a sheep. Or again, young children were sent to work in the coal-mines in the nineteenth century. Today no child leaves school until his middle or late teens.

The balance sheet is difficult to assess in an age which cannot agree on what is 'good behaviour' or 'morality'. But clearly there is change—significant change—in men's ideas about their standards of behaviour towards each other and in the sources from which those standards are derived. It is a change which must have profound consequences for education which, in its concern with man in society, must necessarily be concerned with the rules he adopts to guide his personal relations. And if those rules are now worked out in each man's inner citadel for himself, the contents of the citadel are extremely important, if society is not to become a harsh and brutish context for our living.

In Britain, the attitude of the state towards religious teaching has passed through three stages. Before 1870 religion and education were regarded as inseparable. Most of the schools were established by the two denominational societies and based their curriculum firmly on instruction in the Christian faith. But interdenominational quarrels severely limited their growth and development. All too often denominational interests were paramount over those of the child. The Forster Act of 1870 made an important change which is well summarised by Mrs. Cruikshank—

'Before that date (i.e. 1870) the Central Government had a positive regard for the teaching of religion and had in fact insisted that there was no education without religion. Now, and for three-quarters of a century, it assumed a negative attitude and confined its interest to the sphere of secular instruction.' (*History of Church and State*, Macmillan, 1963.)

This does not mean, of course, that religious education disappeared from the schools; the strong religious and pastoral sense of the teachers and the School Boards saw to that. But it did mean that the state ceased to take any positive interest in it, apart from insisting that it must not be distinctive of any particular denomination. Payment by Results applied only to secular subjects, but religious education went on, closely intertwined with moral education in the minds of almost everybody and it was almost always strongly biblical because it was felt that the 'straight' exposition of the Bible was 'safe.' It is important to remember that religious instruction of some kind was practically universal right up to 1944.

The Act of 1944 marked the resumption by the state of the positive interest in religious instruction which had been abandoned in the 1870 Act, which left it entirely in the hands of the School Boards. It was in some ways a treaty marking the end of the denominational strife which had led to this temporary abandonment

and which had so often hampered educational progress in the nineteenth century. But, as is clear from the speeches made at the time,
the Act also bore witness to a widespread desire for moral and spiritual renewal of the nation during the period of prolonged crisis
in the war—

> 'We today have the responsibility for laying the foundations
> for the nation's future. As the reforms are made effective . . .
> we shall develop our most abiding assets and richest resources—
> the character and competence of a great people.' (Mr. R. A.
> Butler, Hansard, 19 January 1944 [Col. 232].)

The Butler Act placed upon local education authorities an obligation to provide religious instruction and a daily act of worship in all
maintained schools, with provision for both parents and teachers
who wished to do so to opt out of either—or both. It also devised
rather complicated machinery for the preparation of an Agreed
Syllabus for the instruction.

The fact that this settlement has stood the strains of twenty-five
eventful years and has proved sufficiently flexible to accommodate
quite radical developments in the subject during that period,
admittedly on occasion by turning a blind eye to the letter of the law,
shows that its basic principles were sound. However, the fact that
major social and educational changes have taken place since 1944
means that it is now necessary to look carefully at the settlement of
that year to see if any administrative changes, or changes in the
practice of the schools, are necessary to bring it into line with these
developments.

Most of the social and educational changes are for the better.
The first one, which is obviously for the better, is the development
of much more cordial relationships between the different churches
than seemed possible in 1944, let alone in 1870. The Christian
churches are no longer arrayed in embattled positions against one
another, but in matters of religious education speak increasingly
with a common mind and purpose. For this we must be grateful to
Pope John, the Ecumenical Movement, the Vatican Council and to
the quiet initiative of many ministers and congregations. Perhaps we

should not forget also the influence of the much maligned Agreed Syllabus itself, which certainly helped Christians of differing backgrounds to see how much they had in common. In fact the very success of the Agreed Syllabus has largely removed the need for it!

Teachers will, however, continue to need some positive help in the teaching of religion even though it may no longer be necessary to plot a course between the rocks and shoals of allegedly denominational teaching. This guidance might well offer both suggestions for implementing the newer approaches and reference material to ensure a supply of up-to-date information. It will certainly need to take account of local conditions for the greatest need of all is to give the teaching relevance both to the needs of society and to the needs of individual children.

But guidance, if it is to be effective, must be revised constantly, and brought up to date, for the second area of change is in our understanding of the way in which children apprehend moral and spiritual truth. There has been a great deal of research on religious and moral education in the past ten years. Its effects are being more and more widely seen in the content of religious education and in teaching methods in the schools—and, indeed, in the use of the term 'religious education' instead of 'religious instruction.'

The work on the child's moral development owes much to the earlier work of Piaget, but perhaps the greatest contribution has been made by Goldman in his *Religious Thinking from Childhood to Adolescence* (Routledge & Kegan Paul, 1964) which applied Piaget's theory on the development of thinking in childhood to religious education. He demonstrated in particular that the last of the three stages—intuitional, concrete operational and abstract operational— is not usually reached until the mental age of 12 or 13—hence the futility of presenting abstract theological concepts to young children—

'The mark of the true teacher is knowing what not to say. Ruskin says "the only art is to omit" and a greater than Ruskin said, "I have many things to say unto you, but ye cannot hear them now".' (E. F. Braley, *Sunday School Teaching*, Macmillan & Co., 1926.)

E

This research was published in the midst of mounting and incontrovertible evidence that the post-1944 non-doctrinal biblical teaching based on an Agreed Syllabus was not only not working, but was actually counter-productive. Young children were acquiring quite serious misconceptions from Bible teaching which bore no relation to their little worlds. Teenagers were also abandoning the whole idea of religious belief—and the moral teaching with which it was associated—as so much gobbledegook. The baby was thrown out with the bath water. In all too many schools the literal intent of the framers of the 1944 Act was still being carried out—and frequently still is! As a result religious *instruction*—for this is what it was—not only was not strengthening the moral fibre of the nation but was probably weakening it. The Sheffield Institute of Education report of 1961, Loukes's *Teenage Religion* (S.C.M. Press, 1961) and Acland's *We Teach Them Wrong* (Gollancz, 1963) demonstrated beyond doubt that a new approach was needed if religious teaching was to retain any credibility for modern young people.

Goldman embodied his research findings in his *Readiness for Religion* (Routledge & Kegan Paul, 1965)—the dominant theme of which is the need to link religious education with life situations based on the pupil's own interests and experience, so that it may be meaningful to him both at his own personal level and at the level of the corporate life of the community. Loukes advocated a similar problem-centred approach at the secondary stage.

If religious education has nothing to say to a child about the problems—often terrifying problems—which confront him, it may as well be dropped from the curriculum. There should never have been any question of a divorce of religion from real life but, unhappily, there has been in the minds of both children and adults. It is significant —and heartening—that the new I.L.E.A. syllabus is called *Learning for Life*, and equally encouraging that a number of local education authorities are using it as a basis for their own syllabuses.

A simple but cogent analysis of the work of Goldman and Loukes was made in evidence submitted to the Gittins Committee by the Christian Education Movement in Wales, which neatly summarised the negative side of the research by saying that 'the attempt to confine religious instruction to the imparting of scriptural knowledge in the formal situation has rendered this instruction largely ineffectual in raising moral standards and deepening Christian belief.' It then gave a clear account of current research, not omitting some justifiable criticisms and emphasising, quite rightly, that the results demanded not, as some at that time claimed, the virtual exclusion of the Bible from the primary school, but rather a deepened consideration of its place and authority. Finally, it said that the dominant theme of its evidence was 'the need to link Religious Education with life situations; such a theme involves the whole personality and becomes meaningful to both pupil and teacher.'

At the same time as the development of this new approach to religious education, the Farmington Trust was established at Oxford under John Wilson to conduct a ten-year research project on moral education. Its first publication was *Introduction to Moral Education* (Penguin, 1967). It develops the concept of the morally educated man—'Farmington Man'—who has understanding of his acts, their context and their ends, as opposed to the morally trained man who merely conforms to a code without understanding or care. It is the difference between education and instruction. Some instruction may be involved in education, but to define education as instruction is quite inadequate and unacceptable today. This applies as much to religion and morals as it does to physics, French or mathematics.

This research into the foundations of moral behaviour, like that of the Schools Council Moral Education Project, has proceeded on objective and scientific lines, but it has not excluded religious considerations when the logic of the argument has demanded their inclusion—although as Professor M. V. C. Jeffreys has pointed out in *Truth is not Neutral* (Religious Education Press, 1969), religion receives comparatively little mention in Mr. Wilson's 450-page book.

Coincident with the growth of our knowledge of the moral development of children, the explosion of the new theology and the secularisation of society, there has been a quite remarkable growth of social consciousness among young people—one of the bright and shining features in the past decade.

It may, of course, sometimes show itself in inconvenient ways but it is particularly and most positively seen in the remarkable development of Voluntary Service at home and overseas as well as in the range of social activities of some of our schools, colleges and universities, and in the less public, but still deeper, commitment of a steady stream of young people to training for careers which will be for the social betterment of their own or other countries. Of course, by no means all this commitment to working for others can be seen as Christian commitment. Some critics have seen it as an externalisation of conscience, as an attempt to put the world right instead of putting oneself right. Of course many engage in it without any idea of their motives at all—but does this matter? After all, who are we to question their motives? And can we doubt that even unclear motives may still be leading a young person in the right direction?

Many youngsters who are not ready for commitment to Christianity find in community service a satisfying commitment to humanity and perhaps to an unknown and dimly acknowledged ideal of 'the good.' Acland pointed out long ago that the first real commitment for young people is often the decision to say 'Yes' to life rather than 'No.' Today's young people who are saying 'Yes' to life in such a heartening way are surely at least halfway to faith. After all, their spiritual growth will not cease when they leave school, and we may hope that if they now feel that faith without works is clearly dead so they may in time realise that works without faith can be dead also. 'The understanding of life comes before the formulation of theology' (Professor M. V. C. Jeffreys, *Truth is not Neutral*, The Religious Education Press, 1969.)

The splendid body of young people who offer themselves for community service of one kind or another includes those who call themselves Christians, those who call themselves humanists, those who prefer some other title, and maybe some who are simply trying to sort out their own attitude to life and human need. But in activity of this kind the Christian and the non-Christian can work side by side without compromising their beliefs. It is good that this should be recognised and that whatever their motives and beliefs they should discuss them between themselves, which is what young people will almost certainly do.

This thoroughly healthy and desirable growth of social consciousness among children and young people, and its expression in voluntary community service—both in school and outside—surely offers a pointer to all engaged in education as to the direction in which moral education should look. It should be intensely practical and related to life—the child's life. It is also an aspect of education in which both the Christian and the non-Christian teacher can work together in good faith even though—as in voluntary service—one may base his concern on Christianity and the other on love of humanity.

And, after all, by the very nature of his calling, every teacher—whatever his subject—accepts profound moral responsibility for his pupils. This is a responsibility which no teacher—Christian, humanist or agnostic—can escape. Young people of differing beliefs or none, working voluntarily on a community service project, can pool their effort for the good of their fellowmen and a school staff with a similar diversity of belief can pool their effort for the moral development of their children.

The moral and religious development of the child is the concern of every teacher, but it is also the concern of every subject in the curriculum, as it is of the whole corporate life of the school. Truth can be found in Art and Mathematics as well as in the subject labelled 'R.E.'

If God is truth, beauty and goodness, as Plato and St. Paul said (Philippians, iv. 8), He is to be sought in every human activity.

There are many in education who believe that moral education should be left to emerge from the ethos of the school—in particular its personal relationships—and from the formal religious education and the act of worship. But this is not enough. It is to ignore the changes in belief and in the nature and sources of morality which have been discussed in this chapter. Of course the quality of the school's communal life, the personal relations between pupils, between staff and pupils, and, not least, between the staff themselves, are of very great importance.

Every child needs an atmosphere of love and security if he is to grow up capable of responding to and loving others. Many cases of juvenile delinquency are traceable to lack of affection at home and school. It is the context for moral, spiritual and emotional growth during a large part of the child's waking day. Of course, correction and guidance may be necessary, but the important point is that they must be given in a spirit of love and respect for the personality of the child.

But more is needed. There should also be opportunity for discussion of specific moral issues—not sermonising—Heaven forbid!—and not abstract ethics. Both would leave the child untouched. What is needed is the vigorous and uninhibited exploration of actual situations within the child's own experience and interest where a moral issue is involved—when all the facts and all the consequences of this action or the other can be faced and when perhaps rules of behaviour can emerge.

There are those who see moral education as an alternative to religious education but the new approach to religious education pioneered, among others, by Goldman and Loukes, and our new knowledge about moral development in children, do not point to a dichotomy—indeed quite the reverse. They hold out hope for an increasingly fruitful dialogue between the two to the great benefit of the schools and society. Some indication of the hopefulness of this dialogue is seen in a pamphlet issued by a group of humanists and Christians under the editorship of Howard Marratt, and in a recent report on moral and religious education by the Social Morality Council.

The content of the period (or, one would hope, periods) labelled 'Religious Education,' should be very much wider than the retelling of Bible stories (though that has a place) and should certainly not be identified with the inculcation of authoritarian dogmas. Nevertheless, it is unthinkable that the education of our children should ignore the Judaeo-Christian heritage which has played such a dynamic role in our civilisation or the life and teaching of Christ or the development of the church. Its purpose clearly is to help the pupil to consider as deeply as possible the ultimate questions posed by human existence, by his own existence, and then to face them with a faith which is his own because it is freely chosen. And, after all, there is no other kind of faith.

It is safe to assume that Parliament in 1870 did see religious instruction in terms of the inculcation of authoritarian dogmas—hence their nervousness about it. And the very institution of the Agreed Syllabuses indicated that such views were still widespread in 1944, even though the breadth of the settlement then reached indicated that more liberal influences were also abroad. That settlement, has proved fertile ground for the healthy development of religious instruction, which has turned by almost imperceptible stages into the religious education which we know today. Gradual though the changes may have been, it is evident that there is a real difference between the atmosphere of today and that of 1944, still more that of 1870.

On all sides there is an obviously humble and sincere search for truth in the interest of the truth itself, of the pupils and of the nation. Teachers are increasingly beginning to regard themselves as searchers after the truth with their pupils. An impressive consensus is emerging that the object of religious education is to be seen not in ecclesiastical or evangelical terms, but in educational ones in the broadest sense. This means that its object is essentially that of education as a whole.

If it sets out deliberately to ensure that the child believes what we think he ought to believe, it must fail. Its approach throughout must be open. The child should be able to stop in his tracks at any point and say: 'Well, is there a God?—or is it all a lot of bunk?' Its purpose should be to enable him to decide what, if anything, he wants to believe or worship. Like all education, it should help the young to grow into whole, mature people at one with themselves, able to develop good relations with others and capable of responding to God.

Even in our increasingly secular society a great many people still believe that there is a spiritual dimension to human life. One of the objectives of religious education is to create an awareness of it and to provide the opportunity for its growth.

It is also important that religious language and symbols should be understood for they are necessary to the formulation of a coherent faith and the understanding of the faith of others. Perhaps, above all, it should provide a relaxed context of experience—free from coercion or restraint, in which the claims of Christianity can be examined face to face and free decisions made. The British Council of Churches has summed it all up: '. . . the aim of religious education . . . is to deepen understanding and insight, not to proselytize'.

But a word of warning is necessary about the need to avoid proselytizing. What is the teacher to do about his own religious beliefs —or doubts? Conceal them in pursuit of objectivity and neutrality and to avoid indoctrination as suggested by John Wilson, or honestly reveal them in pursuit of truth as suggested by Professor M. V. C. Jeffreys? Clearly it is impossible to reconcile the view that religious education is a quest for truth by teacher and pupil with the concealment by the teacher of his concept of truth—no matter what his motive may be. Deception and untruth cannot ever be a path to truth. If religious education is to retain its place as part of education it must, above all things, be honest.

The obverse of the teacher's right, indeed his duty, to be completely honest is his respect for the intellectual freedom of his pupils. If he has the duty to make his own position clear, his integrity will be respected only if he accords an equal respect to that of his pupils to accept or reject and decide for themselves. This regard for the truth and for personality is perhaps the most important element in religious education. It is also inherent in the teacher's general professional commitment.

Christians may see the two as secular versions of the two great commandments; others may see them as moral imperatives of another kind, but all should be able to accept them.

Applying these criteria the teacher may well feel that he is bound never to teach as true what he believes to be false, that he must make a clear distinction between matters of belief and matters of generally accepted fact, and that he must not suppress legitimate questioning by the weight of his authority, but that he must rather teach in such a way that pupils are encouraged to explore and go on exploring for themselves the great questions which face young and old alike—though undoubtedly in different forms at different stages in life.

If, as is now widely agreed, the purpose of religious education is to introduce pupils to the religious interpretation of life in an informed manner and in such a way that they may be helped to find a way of life for themselves, it cannot be confined to the merely factual but, as Professor Ninian Smart has reminded us, must transcend the historical and try to convey in a sensitive manner what a faith or a way of life means to those who hold it, including the teacher. In this country the basis of such education will clearly be Christianity, but because of the very nature of Christianity other views of life should certainly be included if the pupil is honestly to be prepared for the modern world. It would appear, perhaps paradoxically, that in such an open atmosphere, when all beliefs are open to examination, the Christian faith may be expounded more clearly than before, just because it is recognised that no-one need pretend to beliefs which he does not hold.

Many problems facing religious education lie at the very heart of the whole field of education. Their solution will demand all the thought, skill and devotion we can bring to them. But there is a new feeling of hope. We are learning a great deal about the way in which children approach religious and moral questions. New relationships between religious and moral education are being worked out. The position of religious education in a multi-cultural society is seen more clearly and, most hopeful of all, we at last are beginning to understand that there need be no conflict between commitment and objectivity.

5

Democracy

John Dewey, the great American educator, called his introduction
to the philosophy of education *Democracy and Education*. A recent
Penguin Book of wide-ranging essays on education edited by David
Rubinstein and Colin Stoneman is called *Education for Democracy*.
Both titles are apt, for there is a close affinity between democracy
and education—indeed they are essentially the same process. The
educator's clear responsibility for the quality of the society which
employs him and for the safeguarding of the integrity and importance of the individual is at one with the democratic ideal of a society
where all its members are esteemed, all share in its good and all
participate in its government.

Often the schools, and almost always the so-called democratic
states, fall far short of this ideal. Democracy to many—too many—is
a system of government and nothing more. The purpose of this
chapter is to look first at this narrow concept and then at the wider
meaning of democracy without which the first is inadequate to the
point of being scarcely worth the trouble it takes to organise.

Since the war-created impetus to reform petered out in the early
1950's, disillusion with democracy and scepticism about its ability
to bring home the bacon, to solve the problems which the age of
technology is throwing up, are only too obvious. The percentage
turnout at General Elections—since the second world war—may be
some evidence of this—

1945—75·5	1959—78·7
1950—83·6	1964—77·1
1951—81·9	1966—75·8
1955—76·8	1970—72

In local government elections the figures are even lower, and it is at this level that almost every decision has an immediate impact on the lives of the electors. Clearly, increasingly large numbers of people do not feel it worth while to use their vote.

The 'in' word of the moment, 'participation,' is symptomatic of the feeling that the democratic system of government means little more than electing representatives every few years, in whose selection most people have no say whatever, and then once they are elected, decision making is removed from the electors, becomes quite remote and is often inexplicable to them. The unease about the remoteness of decision making is seen among Members of Parliament themselves. They too feel that the vast majority of decisions are made by the executive in secret and that they are nothing much more than an elaborate franking machine. It is to combat this and to involve the backbencher more that the House of Commons is experimenting with Select Committees on specific departments of state. There is a widespread feeling in Britain that everything is 'fixed' anyhow—so why bother to try to influence the decision?

Secondly, as the scope of both local and national government extends to cover widening fields of social, industrial and economic activity it is quite inevitable that the decision-making in which public representatives are involved becomes limited to major issues. A vast and increasing range of decisions on subsidiary matters, which often have a bigger impact on everyday life than the major ones, is left to the bureaucracy—Whitehall or Town Hall.

Figures of Statutory Instruments
1969   1,902
1970   2,042
(At least 25 per cent of each total were local orders.)

With the best will in the world neither Parliament nor the ministers in charge of the departments concerned, can scrutinise the mass of new law (for that is what it is) as it ought to be scrutin-ised. In effect, a great volume of law is churned out constantly by anonymous officials. Fortunately we are blessed in this country with a Civil Service of impeccable integrity and the highest sense of public duty. Were it otherwise the alarming growth of delegated legislation would be one of the most dangerous trends in our democracy. But it probably contributes in some degree to the grow-ing disillusion with democracy.

A third factor is the cart and horse speed of democratic decision making in the jet age. Oddly enough, technological development itself has slowed it down still further. As the Fulton Committee of Enquiry into the Civil Service pointed out, the use of the computer in government departments now enables greatly increased amounts of data to be taken into account in arriving at decisions (Cmnd. 3638). This, as well as the growing complexity of major decisions, delays the conclusions. Parliamentary and local government pro-cedures look to the young people of today—reared on instant coffee, instant music, instant everything—like the mill-wheel on the Village Green when they ought to be functioning like efficient dynamos serving an age of speed and change.

But perhaps the most potent source of scepticism is our failure to democratise industry or the social structure. Political democracy without either industrial or social democracy is regarded by the young as a circus to placate the natives.

Decisions taken by the boards of industrial companies on such matters as pay and conditions of employment, the location of indus-try, rationalisation, redundancy, etc., may have the most profound effects on the life of the worker and his family. He may find himself moved to the other end of the country without warning or discus-sion. Or he may become redundant after long years of service because of board decisions. He has no power to influence the board —except through his union, and this will not amount to much with the giant, often multi-national, undertakings of today. Its members will almost certainly be unknown to him, and will prob-ably be geographically completely remote. It will also be, in effect, a self-perpetuating board for the Annual Meeting cannot by any stretch of imagination be regarded as democratic—not least because while those who invest their money in the company may vote, those who invest their labour may not. The growing practice of issuing non-voting shares removes even the pretence of democracy.

Little wonder that with the enormous power of the unknown, self-appointed board over the lives of millions of people there should be disillusion with democracy. To most workers today the government of the board-room is more important than that at either Westminster or the Town Hall.

Similarly, in our social structure, wealth is still distributed grossly inequitably and its possession bears little relation to merit or service to the community. We have certainly a more open society than we had in the nineteenth century, but the old class structure remains in spite of this welcome change. (See Chapter 6.) This is seen nowhere more dramatically than in education—

'Middle class pupils have retained, almost intact, their historic advantages over the manual working-class . . . nearly half the lower manual working-class pupils of high ability have left school before they are sixteen-and-a-half years.' (J. W. B. Douglas, *All Our Future*, Peter Davies, 1968.)

New evidence is constantly coming to light of the persistence of the class structure with its privileges largely intact, e.g. the Fulton report referred to above commissioned Dr. A. H. Halsey of Oxford University to carry out a sociological survey and he found that the educational and social base of the administrative class of the Civil Service had scarcely changed during the past 25 years. The problems which social class poses for education are discussed in Chapter 6. The point to be made here is that its persistence with all the consequences of privilege which attach to it is not, to say the least, conducive to a belief that democracy cares equally for all its citizens and enables each one to make the fullest contribution of which he is capable to the common good.

The western democracies, in the main, mock the word. Their democracy is only vote deep. Most of their industry is completely undemocratic, and their societies set greater store by wealth, position and class than they do by service to the community. Little wonder that the term 'democracy' is held in such low regard— except by those who wish to use the pretence that we have it in order to preserve the industrial, social and educational status quo.

The purpose here, however, is to discuss the educational conse- quences of the disenchantment and not the industrial and social reform which is needed to give democracy greater reality. But if education is concerned with the quality of life it must be concerned with all the elements which go to make up 'society' and one of the more important is the mechanism for making decisions which affect the whole or a substantial part of it, i.e. with the way in which it and its institutions are governed. The nature of this mechanism and its effectiveness affect the quality of life for a number of reasons, the most obvious of which is that the decisions made, whether they be new policies or solutions to old problems, may directly affect the lives of a great many people. But not least among them is that most decisions of central and local government as well as of the governing bodies of institutions involve constraints which we accept or freedom which we surrender in return for the security which communal life gives.

Human beings have an inherent desire for a degree of freedom which is unattainable in modern society and the more complex society and technology become the more unattainable the individual freedom man craves.

One need only look at the motor-car—to find an illustration of a piece of modern technology which has extended freedom in many ways but has limited it in others—particularly in the new laws which have been necessary to enable us to have it and survive. A quite different example of growing constraint would be the way in which the concept of ownership of land has been diminished. Planning legislation, powers of compulsory purchase, legal decisions such as that in Rylands v. Fletcher or Tulk v. Moxhay, nationalisation of mineral rights, etc., have reduced it to a shadow of its former self. But few would question that the landowner should not be able to prevent, say, the rehousing of slum families or the building of a by- pass in order to relieve an impossible situation in the High Street.

The constant—and increasing—erosion of individual freedom in order to preserve as much freedom as possible for the greatest possible number is a worrying aspect of modern government. It would be easy for it to degenerate into the filching of the freedom of some class of individuals without a compensatory extension of freedom for many more. The decision to take away an individual's right to choose for himself is so serious a matter in modern society that, clearly, there must be some greater gain elsewhere as a result of it and, above all, he must feel that his view is fully taken into account in making the decision. The feeling that individual choice and freedom is being reduced by 'them,' not by 'us,' in order to create a common freedom, adds much to the disillusion with democracy.

The technique of democracy, in the narrow sense, has two elements, viz. individual decision on a question and the counting of heads.

But, of course, unless the first element is sound, the second is worthless. The counting of heads irrespective of their contents does not necessarily give the right answer. If it does it can only be by chance, and it would merely be a variant of the theme that might is right.

We pay a great deal of very commendable and scrupulous attention to the mechanism, the voting procedure, but precious little to ensuring the soundness of the decision on which it is based. Indeed some political manifestos do their best to make certain that it is not soundly based! In order to be sound there must, first, be adequate information. The importance of providing the data may be so self-evident as to appear hardly worth stating, yet decisions are taken constantly in both local and central government, in elections and throughout the whole field of democratic decision-making, upon quite insufficient information, e.g. the man who relies for his information on a single popular newspaper cannot be fully informed about the great issues of the day.

But an informed democracy is not enough. There is a second requirement—the ability, and courage, to face *all* the facts about a given problem, weigh them one against another and arrive at a sound conclusion. Judgment also is involved, and is as important as information.

Some decisions are very simple, for example, the committee of the local football club deciding whether to raise the subscription to the club. Others are extremely complex, e.g. the decision which every citizen of this country ought to make as to whether or not Britain should join the E.E.C. But the process is the same—assemble all the relevant information, ponder and weigh it objectively, reach a conclusion, count the heads. Only when the whole process takes place is there a reasonable prospect that the right decision will be reached.

If we could ensure that the whole process occurred whenever decisions had to be made we should do much to restore the vitality and credibility of democracy. It is here that education can make a major contribution. If we can inculcate the habit, for that is what it should become, of seeking *all* the facts about a problem, not just the ones which suit our, perhaps pre-conceived view, facing them courageously and objectively, weighing them carefully before reaching a solution, our pupils will gain more and democracy will gain more than they would from all the dull lessons in civics with which the last generation, as well as some of the present, were burdened.

But, of course, drawing a conclusion from the data is the basis of all sound teaching as well as of democracy. How sensible it would be to replace more widely some of the activity which passes as mathematics with logic, as Dr. Z. P. Dienes of the University of Sherbrooke, Quebec, is doing in his Mathematics Programme which is the culmination of many years of work in England, Australia, New Guinea, the U.S.A. and Canada. His book *Modern Mathematics for Young Children* (E.S.A.) deals with the use of his logical blocks and *Learning Logic and Logical Games* (E.S.A.) describes the use of his apparatus in introducing logic to young children.

The Open University also is to be congratulated for including logic in its humanities foundation course—not taken to the lengths of complication beloved by the medieval schoolmen but sound training in the ability to draw conclusions and apply them. The process may be set out like this—

$$
\left.\begin{array}{c}
\text{Premises} \\
\text{(i.e. facts about a problem)} \\
\downarrow \qquad \downarrow \qquad \downarrow \\
\text{Conclusion}
\end{array}\right\} = \text{Induction}
$$

$$
\left.\begin{array}{c}
\downarrow \\
\text{Application of conclusion} \\
\text{to a future similar problem}
\end{array}\right\} = \text{Deduction}
$$

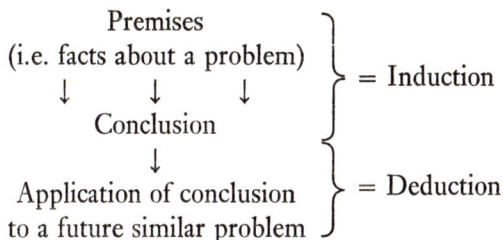

This process of inductive-deductive reasoning will be familiar enough to older generations of teachers and for this reason may be regarded as old hat! But its basic importance to the whole process of learning cannot be over-emphasised. It is without doubt, after the ability to communicate efficiently (see Chapter 8) the most important intellectual skill education can provide.

It is also essential to the efficient functioning of democracy. If, in the above diagram, the term 'premise' is replaced by the words 'Leading article in the *Guardian, The Times, Mirror, Sun, Daily Express, Daily Mail*,' the word 'Conclusion' by 'Individual Decision' and the word 'Application' by 'Vote' its relevance to democracy will be seen.

It is all the more important that the process should become both accurate and habitual because of the rather terrifying development of the communication of ideas in the modern world. We undergo a perpetual bombardment of information, and, all too often, of opinions masquerading as facts. Most insidious of all, we are conditioned to accept assertions, e.g. about the superiority of a product or a policy, by sheer repetition.

In this country we have a small and diminishing number of national newspapers and a considerable range of local or regional ones—all privately owned, all reflecting the views either of their proprietors, e.g. the *Daily Telegraph* or the *Daily Express*, or of their editors, e.g. the Thomson newspapers. Most have firm views about the great issues of the day and there is little doubt that their selection of news bears at least some relation to those views although this varies from one newspaper to another. The reporting of major parliamentary occasions is an example of selectivity in news

F

coverage, determined by the political complexion of the paper. Most of them contain articles which are a mixture of views and news.

However, the old importance of the press as an opinion former has been considerably eroded by the newer media of mass communication—radio and television. Both are in the hands of bodies established by Parliament with a statutory duty to be impartial in the presentation of news and views. As there are at the time of writing about 15·5 million T.V. sets in use in the United Kingdom, the effect must be that the majority of people receive a more balanced view of current problems than when they relied entirely on the press. And, of course, this applies not only to political problems but to the whole range of issues thrown up by modern society—moral, religious, ethical, social, industrial, economic, technological, etc.

A third element in modern mass communication is high-pressure advertising. By definition this must lack objectivity—although it purports to have it in the 'blinding-with-science' type of advertisement which for example examines both brand 'X' and its own product and comes down firmly in favour of the latter. If the development of radio and T.V. with their legal obligations to be objective is a clear gain which has helped to counter the lack of objectivity of a privately owned press, some aspects of the growth and development of modern advertising represent an equally clear loss to the democratic process of informing the public.

It is argued that in the case of both the press and advertising, their multiplicity does ensure a complete picture. Brand 'X' has its own commercial. The *Daily Telegraph* may put a Conservative view but the *Sun* puts a Labour view and the *Guardian* a reasonably impartial one. The person who wishes to take the trouble to look at both points of view will have no difficulty in finding them. This may well be true, but most people read one newspaper and they are attracted to it by features quite other than the views of its proprietor. But because they buy it to read its racing columns or for some other reason, they also see and may acquire a one-sided view of current problems incidentally.

The press, broadcasting and modern advertising certainly give us the potential for a well-informed democracy, but all too often it is misinformed and incapable of making balanced decisions—not because of *lack* of information but because of an excess of propaganda, i.e. information which is less concerned with influencing the conscious mind where reason and judgment can operate upon it, than with influencing the unconscious. One of the less welcome aspects of the development of modern mass media is its increasing use of this technique—influencing the minds of people without their being aware of it. Greatly increased knowledge of psychology has enabled the technique to be improved to the point where educationists can no longer ignore its potency and to the point where they themselves should search their souls about the extent to which educational methods themselves rely on propaganda.

How often in the practice of the schools do we appeal to lower levels of the mind of the child than his reason—rewards, punishments, the use of emotion, letting public opinion in the school do its best—or worst—

'There are vast possibilities of social control in the utilisation of modern techniques of propaganda.' (Professor W. R. Niblett, *Essential Education*, University of London Press, 1947.)

Both parent and teacher use it as ruthlessly in socialising the child as the manufacturer of detergents in selling his product.

The gist of Chapter 4 was that in moral training there should be an appeal to reason and compassion and less emphasis on the conditioning of the child. Unless this is writ large in modern educational practice we shall produce a generation who are merely willing raw material for any charlatan manipulating the mass media to mould as he will. We shall indeed become mere '. . . dupes to crafty rogues.' The individual (in the true sense of the word) cannot survive in the jungle of press, radio, T.V., cinema, mass advertising, unless he is trained to turn the searchlight of reason on all the influences which are battering at him and demanding admission. Nor can any democracy worth the name survive unless its members critically question and examine ideas, information, influences, clamouring for acceptance. But how often the reverse is nearer the truth!—the housewife who falls for the high-pressure advertising of an inferior refrigerator or her husband for an equally shoddy car, the student who follows blindly and without question the campus demagogue, the elector who never tests in his own mind the feasibility or the cost of the political slogan.

If the educator values democracy, as indeed he must if he is concerned with the quality of life, he must recognise in this a major threat to its viability and, ultimately, to its existence. The inter-war European dictatorships assured their take-overs by propaganda before the paraphernalia of terror completed the process. To remind the educational world of this is not to overstate the case, for it is there, in education, perhaps alone, that the creeping danger to the minds of men can be held—and turned. The primary school teacher is more relevant to the defence of democracy than the Prime Minister in the modern world. He and his colleagues alone can ensure its survival.

It is not the purpose of this book to tell the teachers how to do their job, but to point to some of the major problems facing them and to suggest broad solutions. The importance of developing the ability and the courage to find and face all the facts has been mentioned. The equal importance of weighing the facts and reaching balanced conclusions has also been stressed. But this process, familiar enough to the science laboratory, should permeate the whole curriculum—not least the humanities. Its application to moral teaching is obvious. The aim should be that the child should reach a point when he will automatically refuse to generalise—to draw a conclusion—unless he has sufficient evidence. In spite of their shortcomings, indeed because of them, the press, advertising and broadcasting possess great, and largely unused, potential to enable the teacher to develop in his pupils this critical approach to information.

Large comprehensive, secondary and grammar schools are still found where pupils do not have access to newspapers and periodicals. It is almost inconceivable that schools with pupils up to the age of 18 or 16 (and the age of majority is now 18) should not take the national dailies—or such weeklies as *New Society*, *New Statesman*, *The Spectator* and *The Economist*. Of course most of them present biased views and often selective news about current problems, but it is this very characteristic which provides a goldmine of teaching material. Apart from informing pupils about current problems, and this, surely, is of great importance, almost every issue of every newspaper and periodical contains articles which could be examined critically to see whether the information provided is adequate and whether the conclusions are justified. It is difficult to imagine a more useful exercise than an operation of this kind on an *Express* leader. The way in which four or five newspapers deal with the same event or problem can be analysed. What are the facts common to all the accounts? What facts have been omitted from some and how does this affect their conclusions? Taking all the facts common to all the accounts, what conclusion, if any, can be drawn? The possibilities presented by the press for training in a critical approach to the communicators in our society as well as for acquiring an interest in the world outside are enormous.

Nor should the teaching potential of advertising material be ignored. Those L.E.A.'s which refuse to allow it in their schools are just being silly. How can a course in domestic science be regarded seriously if it does not equip a girl to distinguish the wood from the trees in the advertising of domestic products? How can she, when she becomes a housewife, fail to fall for every new line in advertising unless she has a built-in ability to take it apart to see what reality there is in its extravagant claims? But it is not only the housewife who is exposed and vulnerable. All the family need to acquire the habit of saying: 'Well, is that really so? What are the facts on which you base the claim that this product will do what you say?'

And its relevance to democracy?—simply that we must not, we dare not, allow the critical faculty to fall into disuse because of modern advertising techniques. To prevent commercial advertising getting away with it is the surest way to warn the politician off similar techniques. For if he starts to blind us with science, as the detergent manufacturer tries to do, the end of freedom is already in sight. Education must train a generation who will demand from both all the facts about their products and their policies before their claims to support are considered. It is in this that the teachers could

make a major contribution to countering disillusion with democracy
and the danger of the mass media.

Of secondary importance to this, but still extremely important, is
a knowledge of the machinery of democracy. A straight course of
lessons on local government, parliament, elections, etc., is almost
certainly the least effective approach. It is so unrelated to the child's
own experience that he is unlikely to get much out of it—except
boredom which may persist into adult life as an anti-council, anti-
parliament complex. Public representatives are only too familiar
with this attitude!

It makes much more sense to use the annual council elections,
general elections, and the literature they generate, the annual opening of Parliament, parliamentary reports (how many secondary
schools take Hansard?), reports from the local press of town hall
debates, etc. If there is a debate on a slum clearance plan, why not go
to see the area after reading the report? It is also worth remembering
that every school in the country has a number of local councillors
and a Member of Parliament—all of whom would probably be only
too pleased to talk about and discuss their activities. Such initiatives
often lead to a visit to a Council Meeting or even to Westminster
itself. A cup of tea in the House of Commons cafeteria will be an
indelible memory—apart from the unique quality of the tea!

One further point is worth mentioning. All Councillors and M.P.'s
engage extensively in case work. It is more than likely that if the
suggestions on community service in Chapter 7 are followed,
pupils themselves will unearth social problems the solution of which
is beyond them. What a splendid lesson in social responsibility if it
occurred to them to refer these problems to their local council or
parliamentary representative. It would be exactly the kind of response which a living introduction to the machinery of democracy
should evoke.

Similarly, passionate feelings may emerge from a school discussion
group. What a vindication of the school's methods it would be if the
pupils themselves then passed a resolution and forwarded it to the
appropriate quarter!

Thus there is much that education can do to encourage the

balanced thinking without which democracy is extremely vulnerable, to evoke a critical but lively interest in current affairs and the
way they are presented by the mass media and to relate the often
remote mechanism of democracy to everyday life.

But much more, very much more is needed if democracy is to
mean anything more than a type of machinery for making decisions.
There is inherent in the counting of heads an assumption that they
are of equal worth. We mouth this assumption with our lips and
deny it both in our education system and in society itself. The one
reflects the other. An undemocratic society needs an undemocratic
education system to sustain it. If we could change the education
system's undemocratic features we should have taken a long step
towards changing society itself. Those who still believe that we have
an education system which regards all children as being of equal
importance, less able as well as more able, working class as well as
middle class, would perhaps do best to read *The Home and School*
by J. W. B. Douglas (Macgibbon & Kee, 1964) and its sequel—*All
Our Future* by Douglas, Ross and Simpson (Peter Davies, 1968).
These contain the results of probably the most impressive educational survey ever undertaken in this country. They contain incontrovertible evidence of gross injustice to large numbers of our
children, and it is injustice which is unavoidable so long as the
education system is required to preserve an élitist society.

Not unnaturally, those who wish to preserve élitistism, i.e. those
who have arrived and those who hope to do so often vehemently
oppose any democratisation of education. Those who wish to accord
to children the dignity of being treated as intelligent human beings
with wills, minds and souls of their own are dubbed 'progressives'
and that is equated with decadence and permissiveness. The three
Black Papers are an example of a frenzied defence of the undemocratic *status quo* by publications which, to say the least, reflect no
credit on their editors and little on some of their contributors.

But Cox and Dyson are not the only defenders of the *status quo*.
There are those local Councillors, and some Ministers, who blandly
ignore the meaning of English words when they say they want
comprehensive schools but also to retain the grammar schools!

There are parents, fortunately a diminishing number, who support a patently unjust system because they want their children to get on the bandwaggon of the élite. There are a minority of teachers who prefer the relative security and predictability of an authoritarian education system where children are seen and rarely heard (except when they chant their tables), where everyone does as he is told— child by teacher, teacher by head, head by L.E.A., where no parent questions the superior wisdom of the L.E.A. in its diagnosis of what is best for his child, where the clever inherit the earth and the rest are trained to become hewers of wood and drawers of water.

But the winds of change are blowing through society and they must blow through the schools and colleges as well. We must begin to educate for democracy and not for an élitist system, whether it be aristocracy, meritocracy, or plutocracy, a society in which personal worth is esteemed more than birth, wealth, class, colour, creed or position.

Central to our system has been, and often still is, a superiority-inferiority assumption. The minority are superior not only in their degree of ability but also in their kind of ability and must have the best education. The majority are inferior in both degree of and kind of ability and require a different education. This assumption underlies both the practice of streaming and the tripartite, or, more often, bipartite system of secondary education. It is also difficult to avoid the conclusion that, in many minds, it is the rationale of the tripartite system in higher education—universities, polytechnics, and colleges of education.

It is also closely related to the examination system—those who can clear the hurdle of 'O' may try the hurdle of 'A' and those who, by one means or another, get over that may enter higher education. Those judged superior by ridiculously limited criteria at a given moment in a constant process of growth and development do indeed inherit the earth.

The superiority-inferiority assumption is also the starting point of the reasoning which leads to the annual ritual of speech-day. The prize-winners are publicly acclaimed by parents, staff, govern-ors and, indeed, their colleagues. Fine for the winners as they blushingly carry away their shiny new volumes, but what of the majority who do not win? They have been labelled 'non-winners' just as surely and as damningly as the primary school child who has been labelled 'B' or 'C.' A preparation for life which has its winners and losers? Of course it not only prepares for, but it preserves, the kind of society in which we live, a society which says it esteems all its members equally but, in fact, does no such thing. If educationists merely see their function as the preservation of society as it is, just or unjust, they will continue all the indignities and injustices which at present deface the system. On the other hand, if they accept a wider purpose, the improvement of society, they will examine every feature of the system, administration, organisation, curricula, method, in the light of the kind of society in which they want their pupils to live.

Fortunately there is now a growing volume of highly reputable educational research to guide them. The National Foundation for Educational Research carried out a survey of teacher attitudes towards research in 1968 and found, among other things, a large expectation of benefits from it in future. This greater and growing willingness of teachers to base their practice on research is one of the more hopeful aspects of the current educational scene. A good deal of the credit for it must go to the N.F.E.R.—not only for the highly relevant projects it has undertaken but also for its efforts to disseminate the results. It also owes a good deal to the perceptiveness and skill of educational journalists both in the educational press and the national and local dailies.

Two examples will suffice to illustrate the extent to which research findings support the plea of this chapter for a more democratic education system. The first relates to the concept of intelligence. At the time of the passing of the Butler Act it was generally believed that intelligence was mainly innate and therefore remained unchanged and unchangeable throughout life. It was impervious to the influence of such major environmental factors as home, school and neighbourhood. It was also believed that it could be quantified accurately and a score, an intelligence quotient (I.Q.), given to every child tested. It was the bedrock of a child's ability and determined his capacity for further learning and development. This nice, tidy theory was carried to its logical conclusion in the use of the I.Q. to decide whether or not the child of 11 would later be able to profit from an academic secondary education, the examinations at the end of which decided whether or not he could profit from higher education.

In the ensuing quarter century a massive amount of research in this country, the U.S.A., Sweden, Germany, and elsewhere has established beyond any reasonable doubt that none of the three premises on which this reasoning was based is tenable. We now know that intelligence grows and is affected by environmental factors from the cradle to the grave. Among these, so far as children are concerned, there is clear evidence that the attitude of the home is by far the most important. Secondly, research has pointed overwhelmingly to the impossibility of measuring the innate part of a child's intelligence without the measurement containing also part of his acquired intelligence—

> 'Knowledge of the genetically-determined innate abilities of his pupils is inaccessible to him (the teacher) and will remain so. . . .
> The search for culture-free, or culture-fair intelligence tests is an illusory one. The effect of environment begins at birth—and may be earlier—so that by the time the child arrives at the gate of the school he may be already heavily handicapped.' (Dr. Stephen Wiseman, Director of N.F.E.R. in an address, 1 December 70.)

The I.Q. is, therefore, not wholly genetic in origin and the genetic part of it cannot be accurately measured. As these two premises have been progressively demolished the third can no longer honestly be maintained. The I.Q. at 11 years of age, or the result of the 11 + selection procedure, is a thoroughly unreliable, and, therefore, grossly unjust, index of a child's ability to profit by a better secondary education and by higher education.

This new knowledge about intelligence is the major part of the educational case for the comprehensive school—a school in which the door to educational opportunity is open throughout, where all share equally in teaching and other resources, a school which is not based on the undemocratic superiority-inferiority assumption, but where children are equally esteemed.

A second area where research is vindicating the efforts of progressive teachers to rid their schools of this assumption is in the gathering movement to end streaming by ability in all schools. This was discussed in Chapter 3. The growing volume of evidence against streaming shows that not only does it not achieve what its supporters claim but that, as was always suspected, it does great and often irretrievable, harm to label a child as inferior, e.g. 'B,' 'C,' 'D,' 'E,' etc. Any doubts which remain about the reliability of this conclusion must be removed by the N.F.E.R. report: *Streaming in the Primary School* by Joan C. Barker, Lunn, January, 1970. Where schools persist in streaming, i.e. in basing their organisation on the superiority-inferiority assumption, they are doing so in the face of a wholly convincing volume of research findings. Worse, they are grooming the majority for failure. To stream children by ability in a primary school is an educational outrage of the first order—understandable enough a quarter of a century ago when we knew little of its effects on later development and when class-teaching was the order of the day. But utterly inexcusable today when we know its consequences on both secondary stage progress and vocational opportunity and when the class lesson has been almost universally replaced by individualised teaching.

And so, education is concerned with the vitality of democracy far beyond improving the technique of decision-making, far beyond an intelligent knowledge of current affairs. The pattern of the education system, the organisation within its institutions, their curricula and their methods of teaching should be entangled beyond separation with the values upon which a true democracy would be based. There is an urgent need to change them all not only because by so doing we may create a better society, but because dignity and esteem are the birthright of every child.

6

Social Class

In spite of the growing openness of our society and the lip service we pay to democracy we still present a picture of a social pyramid divided longitudinally into strata which attract wealth, influence, privilege and esteem in inverse proportion to their size, i.e. diminishing from the small apex to the large base. The assumption underlying this structure is very similar to the superiority-inferiority assumption on which our education system is still largely based. Near the apex, there is a relatively small but growing group of people—the upper middle class—who have the highest incomes, luxurious well-equipped homes, send their children to public schools and the universities, occupy the commanding heights in business, the law, the public service, politics, the armed forces and the Anglican Church, run expensive motor-cars, have weekend cottages, take their holidays in the Caribbean and speak grammatically correct English usually without a regional accent. They are the well-to-do business and professional men and their families.

At the base there is the large but decreasing lower working class with the lowest income groups, often living in sub-standard rented accommodation in which facilities such as baths and toilets may be shared, or in council houses, sending their children to the neighbourhood school which may often be as sub-standard as the housing around it, leaving school at 15 and rarely going into further or higher education, owning perhaps a jalopy but more often relying entirely on public transport, taking their holidays at Butlin's—if at all, speaking in regional accents often with a robust disregard for grammar, attracting little esteem and possessing no privilege.

The child from the upper group will have his own bedroom, he will never lack food, clothing, light or heat, he will possess books, games and equipment such as a tape recorder and a record player, he will be almost as much at home at continental holiday resorts as in this country, he will have 'good' table manners and other social graces, he will probably talk freely to his parents—even about such matters as sex—he will rarely be involved in violence, he will not be subjected to the pressure for physical survival and he therefore will learn to become ambitious and defer immediate gratification of his desires in order to achieve more in future. In other words, he will acquire the characteristics of his social group—behaviour, speech, feelings, values and regard them as a civilised way of life.

The child from the lower stratum, on the other hand, will probably share a bedroom—even a bed, he will lack books and a place in which to read quietly, he may never have been to London, his manners—judged by the criteria which apply at the other end of the social scale—may be appalling, he will rarely discuss his activities in or out of school with his parents and will certainly never discuss sex with them, he may be aggressive and often involved in fights, he will always be concerned with physical survival and, because of this, he will gratify desires when he can. He like his more fortunate counterpart will also learn the behaviour pattern and the values of his class and regard them as natural.

Of course, there is no list of characteristics which divide one class from another; nevertheless social stratification into broad socio-economic groups is recognisable—as we often discover when an individual finds himself classified wrongly! The usual broad classification is that adopted by Dr. J. W. B. Douglas in the survey referred to in Chapter 5, i.e. the non-manual workers are divided into upper middle class and lower middle class and the manual workers into upper and lower working classes. The basis of this division—apart from occupation—is the education of the parents and the type of family in which they were brought up. This terminology is illogical for the terms middle class and lower class imply that there is an upper class but today this is scarcely so. The tiny 'upper crust' of landed gentry or aristocracy has diminished in size and influence—except in the ownership of land—to such an extent that it can no longer be called a social class. Most of its members earn their living in business or the professions and are indistinguishable from the growing business and professional class. The stately home has become nothing more than a lucrative tourist attraction and the manor house has probably been divided into flats. The words 'Middle' and 'Lower' themselves are also illogical—as illogical as calling the House of Lords the upper House!

Although the divisions between social classes are diffuse at the margins we still recognise them with little difficulty. But a number of factors in modern society are making recognition increasingly difficult and, indeed, changing the structure both by encouraging vertical mobility within it and by ironing out the class differences. If the democratic open society is a necessary context for the lives of free men and women education must complement these factors by making the classless society a major objective but it does not always do so by any means. This is not a society based upon the view that Jack is as good as his master. After all he may or may not be! It is one in which Jack and his master are equally esteemed—with all that that implies.

The technological revolution has been discussed in Chapter 2. Its most obvious effect is in the transformation of our material lives. The council house of a manual worker may be better equipped and better planned than the Mayfair flat of his company chairman. Mass production of household furniture and equipment, universal hire-purchase facilities, the growth of building societies and local authority house building are all combining to bring high-quality homes within the reach of the manual worker. In the years 1945–70, 3,138,416 private houses and 4,219,369 council dwellings have been built in the United Kingdom.

Dr. Douglas found quite dramatic improvements in the performance of primary school children when they moved from sub-standard accommodation to council houses, e.g. of children with

T scores* of 61 +, 98·3 per cent of those living throughout on council estates were at grammar schools, 88·5 per cent of those moving to council estates and 75 per cent of those living throughout in private dwellings (J. W. B. Douglas, *The Home and The School*, MacGibbon & Kee, 1964 [page 34]). Thus among these children of high ability 23·3 out of every hundred of those living throughout in private accommodation fail to get to the grammar school compared with those living in council houses. There are differences at all levels of ability though they are less marked among the less able. The improvement in educational performance ultimately leads to greater social mobility. The docker's son may get to the university and become a scientist. He will have moved from the base stratum to the apex because his family was re-housed when he was at the primary school.

Another effect of the growth of technology is the growing power of labour because of its shortage and the emergence of larger, often international, industrial units. This has forced up industrial wages and reduced the differential between them and professional salaries. This, together with the development of the welfare state and increasing government intervention over a wide field of national life, has led to a considerable redistribution of incomes and wealth since 1945. As income and wealth are two of the marks of social class their more equitable distribution has blurred the edges of the strata, e.g. before 1939 the holiday habits of social classes were fairly distinct. In the late 1930's the occasional manual worker and his family reached the Rhine or Paris for 7 days, but only the rich basked on the Riviera. Today the beach at Nice is a social cross-section of Europe.

Similarly with clothing—in the past the uniform of social class. It is no longer the case that the duke buys his underpants at Simpson's and the gamekeeper his at Marks & Spencer's. St. Michael has become universal. The class of the shop girl and the debutante are indistinguishable from their clothes. The working-class docker and his middle-class scientist son may buy their suits and shirts at the same shop. This is another distinguishing mark of class which

---

*The T score is similar to the I.Q. but has a mean of 100 and a standard deviation of 10 instead of 15.

is being ironed out by the fairer distribution of wealth, mass production and improved design and materials.

Not least among the consequences of technology is the changing pattern of employment. The labour content of industry is rapidly decreasing both because of automation and as a consequence of the relentless drive to reduce unit costs. As a result the employment prospects for the unskilled are constantly contracting and there are many more people employed in the professions and services. Ten years ago there were 691,400 people employed in coal mining in Great Britain. Today there are 360,100; but the number of teachers and lecturers employed by local authorities increased from 412,086 to 608,449 in the same period. The employment characteristics of class are changing with a reduction in numbers at one end and a corresponding increase at the other.

Apart from the consequences of higher wages, a lowering of differentials and changing employment patterns other aspects of economics are having an impact on the class structure, e.g. share ownership—helped by the unit trust movement—and house ownership are more widely distributed; inflation—a permanent feature in the post-war world—bears least heavily on the group which possesses the greatest industrial power to increase its earnings—the skilled industrial workers; the growth of private pension schemes has divided the large retired population into two classes of their own, fiscal policy has greatly reduced the advantage of inherited wealth and capital gains—two major possibilities in the past for reaping without having sown, paternalism in the boardroom is—under the sheer pressure of competition—being forced to give place to ability.

The mass media is also playing its part in increasing the fluidity of the class structure. Two generations ago the vast majority of the population had never heard a symphony orchestra or seen a play by Ibsen or Shakespeare. Culture was something the upper class had and the working class respected—or suspected—but did not have. Today high-quality drama, music and ballet are on tap in every home. Within the past month of writing this chapter the B.B.C. has broadcast T.V. programmes at peak viewing periods on the life and works of W. B. Yeats and George Orwell.

Patronage of the arts by the central government through the Arts Council and by local authorities through regional arts associations has brought music, drama, ballet, poetry, sculpture and painting to industrial and rural areas which were culturally deprived—though a great deal more resources are still needed to extend this policy to the provinces. Culture is no longer a mysterious aroma surrounding the well-to-do. It is beginning to deepen the quality of life for the manual worker and his family as well.

The media has also enabled the two nations to know more about each other. The professional family in the comfortable home cannot escape from the kitchen sink drama set in down-town Liverpool, and the Tyneside shipyard worker's family is equally familiar with the home and life of the Surrey stockbroker. In the days of the early Forsytes neither end of the social spectrum knew, or cared, much about the other.

Perhaps the last social veil was removed when the entire nation saw a film about the life of the Queen and her family. It destroyed the magic but it revealed a pleasant family of human beings like ourselves—a revelation which must have improved understanding. T.V., radio, press, the cinema are opening vistas through the barriers of class in all directions. This has improved communication and made for a more open society.

In addition to the pressure of technology, economics and mass media there has been the influence of a long period of egalitarian philosophy in politics. The Labour Party came into existence in the early months of the century. Its philosophy was woven from a number of strands—Christian, Fabian, Marxian, Co-operative all bound together by a homespun, indigenous socialism which had emerged from the evils of early nineteenth-century industrialism. Central to all its thinking was—and still is—the ending of social class in so far as it attracted privilege and stood in the way of equality of opportunity. Since its formation it has replaced the Liberal Party as one of the two major parties. Between 1945 and 1970 it has shared power almost equally with the Conservative Party. The Conservative Party itself has changed. The election of a Leader who could say with pride in a T.V. interview that his mother had been 'in service' before her

G

marriage would have been unthinkable even ten years previously. Neither party has made any major onslaught on class barriers—indeed some policies have been designed to reinforce them. Circular 10/70 issued by Mrs. Thatcher, the Secretary of State for Education and Science, is one example. Their influence has come much more from the general acceptance of equality of opportunity and the ending of privilege as major political objectives.

Although for all these reasons the gradual erosion of class barriers continues there are still clearly recognisable class groupings each with its values and standards to an extent which detracts from the quality of our communal life. If community life of high quality is essential to the fulfilment of individuals, education must be concerned about it. But too often its only concern has been to preserve the class structure, to condition its pupils, in the words of the Church Catechism, to ' . . . do my duty in that station of life to which it hath pleased God to call me,' to accept as the natural order of things that we have our superiors who are cleverer, richer, more influential than we are and, because they have these attributes, to regard it as natural that they should have privileges which are not available to the rest of us. Of course the good old Victorian virtues of hard work and ambition were dangled as ladders by which it was just possible to climb up a few notches. Many examples of rags to riches were brought out of the cupboard to prove the existence of the ladders.

The thoroughly undemocratic nature of a good deal of our education system of maintained schools and of their practices was discussed in Chapter 5. It serves to perpetuate social class because it divides mankind into the superior minority and the inferior majority, and the criterion for separating the sheep from the goats is, we are told, intelligence. It is, therefore, highly relevant to any examination of the claims of those who wish to perpetuate this system to look at the connection between measured intelligence and social class for research results into this connection since the war have further exposed the absurdity and the injustice of 11 + selection, grading and similar devices.

The stark fact which has been demonstrated beyond doubt by

Lord Robbins, Dr. Douglas and many others is that working class children are not getting a fair deal from our education system.

Dr. Douglas tested all the children in his survey at the ages of 8 and 11. He found that the children of manual workers at all levels of ability showed a relative decline of performance between the two tests, e.g. among children of high ability with T scores between 56 and 60 upper middle-class children gained 1·52 points between the ages of 8 and 11, lower middle-class 0·62, upper working-class fell by 0·81 and lower working-class by no less than 2·27 points (J. W. B. Douglas, *The Home and The School*, MacGibbon & Kee, 1964, page 47). This progressive deterioration in the performance of working-class children relative to the middle class, which applies both to intelligence and to school performance, means that by the age of 11 the child of the manual worker has fallen behind the child of the middle-class parents of equal ability at the age of 8. The consequence of this is that 54 per cent of upper middle-class children go to the grammar school but only 11 per cent of the children of the lower working class. Great as the social class difference in educational opportunity is at the primary stage it is even more marked in the secondary school. Fewer working-class children stay on at school and gain certificates. This also applies at all levels of ability, e.g. taking the two extremes of both social class and ability, of the children with T scores of 60+, 97 per cent of upper middle class do so and 80 per cent of lower working class, while for those with scores of 44—the range is from 40 per cent to 3 per cent (Douglas, Ross and Simpson, *All our Future*, Peter Davies, 1968, page 204). Nearly half of all working-class children have left school by 16½ years of age. The chances of a working-class child going to the university have not improved, relative to those of the middle-class child, in thirty years.

This major disadvantage still suffered by working-class children is Britain's biggest and most inexcusable brain-drain. It amounts to a colossal failure to develop a vast reservoir of our native ability. A similar failure to exploit economic resources would be regarded as a national disgrace and scandal. To make matters worse, in the independent sector, we cosset mediocre ability by applying to it a quite disproportionate share of national educational resources—

particularly teachers. We dress the geese to look like swans and, by neglect, allow many swans to turn into geese.

This quite deplorable state of affairs is justified by the traditional educationists on the grounds that intelligence is almost entirely inherited, that it is not influenced greatly by environment, that it can be measured reasonably accurately and therefore the measurement (I.Q.) possesses a high predictive quality so far as the child's future development is concerned. Because of all this, the argument runs, the working-class child does less well in tests of ability and attainment simply because his genetic inheritance from his parents is lower. His father is a docker, not because of any shortcomings in our social and educational systems in the past, but because his ability fits him to be a docker and not a scientist. His son will inherit a similar type of ability.

The argument is so demonstrably false as to be almost ridiculous were it not for the fact that it is the rationale for selection at 11+ and all that follows from it. There is no evidence whatever that the inherited ability of working-class children is in any way inferior to that of middle-class children but there is a fair amount of research which indicates otherwise. As Sir Cyril Burt has cast around himself the mantle of High Priest of educational traditionalism it is necessary to look at his theory of intelligence and the more modern view which has developed in recent years. Burt's view of intelligence followed that of Spearman who held that there was an inherited common strand running through all mental abilities but particularly the higher ones such as reasoning, comprehension, judgment, etc. This he called the g factor. Intelligence is then a collection of varied thinking abilities. This view was shared by Professor P. E. Vernon and set out at length in *Educational Research* (November 1958), but, since that time, his views have clearly been modified by the accumulating evidence that environmental factors are a good deal more important than was previously believed. He has also stated in terms the impossibility of quantifying the genetic part of intelligence without at the same time measuring the influence of cultural background.

Burt's evidence in support of his view in which, like Jensen at a later date, he agreed that perhaps 20 per cent of the g factor is determined by environment, is criticised by Lewis Owen and Colin Stoneman in their contribution to *Education for Democracy* (Penguin, 1970). They also refer to Professor D. H. Stott's view that the validity of Burt's conclusion that the individual differences in intelligence depend far more on genetic factors than on environment is invalid without a number of assumptions which Burt has made in his work on identical twins but which are highly dubious, e.g. he made the assumption that twins are typical of mankind in general but there is a fair amount of evidence that this is not the case (*British Journal of Psychology*, November 1966). He also assumed that the pre-natal environment of the unborn child was an unimportant factor in intelligence. Here again, there is growing evidence to the contrary, particularly in relation to dietary influence.

Professor A. R. Jensen in his controversial paper referred to in Chapter 9 concluded that pre-natal influences were probably the largest environmental factor in measured intelligence (*Harvard Educational Review*, June 1969).

In the Teale Lecture to the Royal College of Physicians of London on 23rd October 1969 Professor T. McKeown found a correlation between weight at birth and verbal reasoning scores in the 11 + examination. He presented these findings with very great caution but nevertheless concluded that in the case of low weights at least it was an open question whether weight at birth did affect the scores and, of course, there is a connection between birth weight and social class (*British Medical Journal*, 11 July 1970). 'It may be that when full consideration of peri-natal as well as environmental effects on I.Q. is completed, there will be very little class difference in I.Q. left to be explained genetically.' (Owen and Stoneman, *Education for Democracy*, Penguin, 1970.)

The change in Professor Vernon's view of intelligence is illustrative of the changed view generally and it is upon this, particularly upon the greater emphasis on environmental factors, that the progressive movement in education largely bases its case for radical change in the education system.

Of course there are other theories of intelligence which have gone beyond Professor Vernon's latest view. Broadly the change in thinking is to abandon the g factor concept in favour of a view that intelligence is a bundle of intellectual abilities which are in varying degrees amenable to training but without a common factor. Perhaps the most significant consideration for education in this trend—which does not deny that the separate abilities are probably genetic in origin—is the consequence of a view of abilities which originate not on the periphery of a common g factor but genetically independently. This theory would reduce the use of the I.Q. to predict a child's future development to an absurdity because the I.Q. is a blanket index which presumes to measure the child's total intelligence. If, however, intelligence consists of separate abilities determined independently, influenced constantly by environment from the pre-natal period of life onwards, it follows that one person may possess considerable potential in one or more directions but not in others.

Thus the I.Q. as a predictive instrument may well have built into it a double injustice. We know beyond doubt that a large element in it is a measure of social background but there is now also growing evidence that, because it is a blanket index it cannot reveal special abilities of high quality, indeed it may hide them. There is sufficient evidence of the second of these injustices to underline the gross unfairness of 11 + selection and streaming which follows from the first.

Thus the continued uncritical acceptance of a discarded theory of intelligence by many administrators in the organisation of the educational system, by many head teachers in the organisation of their schools and by many teachers in their teaching methods is a major factor in the preservation of social class. Politicians responsible for national educational policy are little better, e.g. the tripartite system of higher education is as unjust, wasteful and socially divisive as a similar system at the secondary stage. Change in education is slow because, by definition, the system is conservative. There is always a time lag before it responds to change. Unfortunately, in the meantime, its failure to respond quickly enough to the changed view of intelligence is denying to vast numbers of children the opportunities they ought to have and which, in our self-righteous moments, we profess to be giving them.

It is important, however, to look at the whole field of education and see the many hopeful signs of change. Among these the progressive movement in the primary schools which have been liberated from the baleful influence of the 11 + shines like a beacon. Almost all local authorities have either ended or are in process of ending 11 + selection. Tripartite higher education is increasingly questioned. It is unthinkable that the pattern of autonomous universities, local-authority financed and controlled polytechnics and mono-technic colleges of education can continue for long.

There is however, one unique sector of our system in this country which contributes directly and overtly to the preservation of social class which is not changing but is defending itself, its right to exist and its privileges against all comers with some success—the 273 public schools, 2,800 other independent schools and 179 direct-grant grammar schools in England and Wales. This independent and semi-independent sector provides for 7 per cent of all pupils and of these 5·5 per cent are at independent schools of which 3·9 per cent are recognised as efficient. It is somewhat misleading to set out the independent-school population as a percentage of the whole school population as most of their pupils are at the secondary stage and do not enter until the age of 13 years compared with 11 years in the maintained schools. At the age of 14 3 per cent of boys and 2 per cent of girls are in public schools but at the age of 17 the percentages have risen to 12 per cent and 6 per cent respectively. Thus the proportion of children is not large and is falling.

1947—9 per cent of all school children in independent schools.

1957—7 per cent

1967—5·5 per cent

This percentage fall is not merely due to the increased numbers in maintained schools. There has also been a fall in actual numbers, e.g. the number of 14 year olds fell from 47,000 to 37,600 between 1947 and 1967. Nevertheless, in spite of the relative smallness of the independent sector and its gradual reduction in size, it still contains approaching half a million children, mainly fee-payers, who enjoy privileges in their schooling, in their chances of entry into higher education and in their prospects of employment in many fields which are not available to the other 93 per cent of our children. It is perhaps not generally known that the state pays wholly or partly for 10 per cent of all the children (40,000) at independent schools. They are mainly the children of diplomats, officers, etc., serving abroad.

One of the most obvious advantages enjoyed by the independent schools over the maintained schools is the more generous staffing ratios. In 1967 the pupil/teacher ratio in public schools was 11·6 but in maintained grammar schools it was 16·8. Of all the independent schools recognised as efficient compared with the maintained schools the ratios were 12·7 and 23·1. The effect of this and other advantages is seen in the success of the entry of their pupils into the Administrative class (see page 67) and the diplomatic service. The ratio of entrants to competitors in the years 1963–67 was as follows—

	Administrative Class	Diplomatic Service
Public Schools	1:4·6	1: 9·3
Direct-grant Schools	1:4·4	1:10·8
Maintained Schools	1:7·5	1:20·6

Similar advantages are obvious in the destination of school leavers. Of the total number of leavers going to Oxford and Cambridge in 1966, 42·15 per cent were from the independent recognised schools, i.e. from schools catering for 3·9 per cent of the nation's children, and 39·14 per cent from all maintained schools, i.e. from schools catering for 93 per cent of our children. On the other hand, of entrants to colleges of education, the poorest relation in our tripartite higher education system, 6·31 per cent were from the independent schools, 7·83 per cent from the direct-grant schools and 85·87 per cent from the maintained schools.

But perhaps the most telling figures of all are of the leavers going directly into employment, i.e. those who did not enter higher or further education. In 1966 of these, 2·66 per cent were from independent schools, 1·13 per cent from direct-grant schools and 96·2 per cent from maintained schools.

All the above figures are taken from the Public Schools Commission First Report (H.M.S.O.). They reveal a small and diminishing élitist system co-existing with the state system. But while it provides for relatively few of the nation's children it clearly trains them to wield an influence in the life of the nation which is out of all proportion to their numbers or their ability. Bearing in mind that they educate about 7 per cent of our children, they provided over 90 per cent of the Conservative Cabinet in 1963, 20 per cent of Labour M.P.'s in 1966, 70 per cent of our admirals and generals and air chief marshals in 1967, 90 per cent of judges and Q.C.'s in 1967, 80 per cent of the directors of the Bank of England in 1967, and 60 per cent of heads of colleges and professors at Oxford and Cambridge in 1967.

It is difficult to see any validity in our claim to be a democracy when the establishment which directs the life of the nation is drawn to such an extent from a tiny minority not possessed of any special ability but merely of sufficient wealth, or ingenuity, to pay school fees.

There was something to be said in defence of the parent who refused to submit his child to the savage injustice of the local authority 11 + selection procedure, made considerable financial sacrifice and contracted out of the state system. But where selection has been ended there is no longer the need to do this. The reduction in numbers at independent schools may partly reflect this factor but is probably due much more to the increasing burden of paying school fees. However, it is highly improbable that either economics or the growth of comprehensive schools will cause the hard core of major public schools to wither away. Nor is the plan for integration put forward by the Public Schools Commission—First Report likely to achieve this objective, indeed, if adopted, it would almost certainly give them a new lease of life at public expense. But the opening sentence of the Commission's recommendations is incontrovertible in view of the statistics quoted above. 'Our general conclusion is that independent schools are a divisive influence in society.' Of all the aspects of national life the education system, above all, should be concerned with the removal of divisive influences but, as far as these schools are concerned, not only does it not do so but it creates and maintains a major social barrier.

On the other hand, the advance of technology and growing intervention by the central government and public bodies in our lives have made the preservation of individual freedom and choice a major preoccupation of all who are concerned with policy making. One must weigh against the undoubted social divisiveness of the independent-school system and all the inequity which flows from it, the argument that it would be intolerably oppressive in a free society to forbid any parent under any circumstances to educate his child outside the state system—even if the education he provided for his child was as good as that in the state schools and if no part of the cost fell on public funds. The difficulty is, of course, to assess the genuineness of this argument and the extent to which well-to-do parents are concerned with maintaining the privilege, the power and the influence of their class rather than with individual freedom. All too often those who defend the public schools on grounds of freedom of choice are highly articulate in denying it to the 93 per cent for whom the public school is not an option.

An answer must be found. At a time when Britain and other European countries are moving away from a system of secondary education designed for an élite to secondary education for all and when this and other changes are eroding social divisions it cannot seriously be maintained that the independent sector can turn its back and continue to educate an élite selected on the sole criterion of wealth. We should be foolish indeed as well as wrong to continue to exclude the vast majority of our children from a fair chance of reaching the seats of power as we do today. Perhaps the best and most honest answer would be straightforward legislation to forbid anyone outside the state system to conduct a school except under licence and with a licence granted only when the need for it could not be met elsewhere and was demonstrated beyond doubt. A clear break of this kind would be preferable to complicated variants of the Fleming solution of local authorities taking places.

At the same time the public services, particularly the civil service and the diplomatic service, must be much more active in attracting applicants from the maintained schools. A vigorous effort by the central government could divest the public and direct-grant schools of the privileged but quite unmerited position their leavers enjoy at present.

7

Community and Leisure

The desire of human beings for social intercourse with their fellows has been explained in a number of ways. Freud saw sociability as the product of inhibited libidinal impulses. His view was criticised by Suttie (1935) who regarded the capacity to enjoy affection and companionship as an inborn disposition which first manifests itself in the baby's response to his mother. The early twentieth-century psychologists, in particular McDougall and Trotter, attributed it to the herd instinct. Ginsburg (1932) saw its origin in the desire to be socially sanctioned over a wide range of activity, i.e., one's companions in the group are valued for more than the security their presence affords.

Whatever the origin of sociability may be, human beings clearly appear to have three basic social needs. They need the affection of congenial companions, a sense of having a purpose or fulfilling a function within the group and the affirmation of their values by their companions. The lack of any of these is a major social deprivation, e.g. D. W. Harding has quoted in *Social Psychology and Individual Values* (Hutchinson's University Library, 1953) the retired person who feels he no longer has a function in society and the businessman having spent his life in fierce competition with his fellows who tries to return to the simple, congenial relationships of his youth by retiring to his native village.

These needs, if satisfied, keep at bay the inherent insecurity of the human being. Unable to avoid the transitoriness of his humanity he turns to his partners in the human predicament for comfort, identity and approbation. But there is more to man's need of community than his search for security—important though that is. It enables the human predicament to be submerged, to be cut down to size indeed, virtually to be forgotten. Coming face to face with the problems of others corrects the perspective of one's own problem. The irremediable insecurity of life becomes tolerable when its burdens are shared. The sharing and the communication and understanding which accompany it create among a group of persons a corporate identity with a continuing life of its own which is a good deal more than the sum total of all the persons in it. It is not a chain which is as strong as its weakest link but a context in which the weak can be protected, the strong have their strength enhanced, none are isolated, all are secure. It enables all its members to achieve their full personal stature. Nothing which is conducive to the growth of personality can function in isolation—there can be no morality except in relation to other people.

Christ placed the fulfilment of this basic social hunger at the very centre of His teaching 'Love thy neighbour as thyself' was one of the two great commandments, giving oneself for others, service before self, submerging self in order both to live with one's transitory self and with others. This theme was carried to its logical conclusion in the crucifixion.

The idea of salvation through service, suffering and sacrifice is older than man. The creativity of sacrifice, of life born of death is inherent in nature. The young bracken frond pushes up through the decayed remains of other summers; the gaudy flower dies and the fertilised ovary lives, grows and nurtures next year's embryonic bloom; the butterfly lays its eggs and dies; the animal spends itself in the reproduction of its kind. Professor M. V. C. Jeffreys has pointed to the antiquity of the idea: 'One of man's most ancient insights is into the creativeness of suffering and sacrifice, and the idea of life created through death is expressed in myth as early as 6000 B.C.' (*Glaucon*, Pitman, 1950.)

Not the least important aspect of the modern relevance of this ancient insight is the equating of service and freedom. The pre-condition of worthwhile freedom is freedom from oneself—from all the inhibiting anxieties which modern living brings—and this can be achieved only in personal relationships with others. The only freedom worth the name is freedom to grow, fully to establish identity as a person, and this can only be a product of giving. It is the oldest of all illusions that freedom can be achieved by 'getting on,' by winning the pools, by reaching the 'top,' by doing better than the Jones's—an easily understood illusion in a society which persists in regarding the acquisition of wealth and possessions as meritorious.

Thus, healthy communal life in all the groups in which we live our lives is essential to our sense of security, to our salvation from ourselves, to our personal growth and, therefore, to our freedom. The problem today is that so many of the more formative and crea-tive groups are losing their cohesion and therefore their ability to meet our social needs. The family is by far the most important and most threatened. The growing divorce figures were quoted on page 52. They probably indicate greater honesty and greater unity among the marriages which persist but they also mean that there is a rapidly growing number of children living in broken homes.

The influence of television and the working mum as elements inhibiting communication are mentioned in Chapter 8. Anything which weakens communication between the members of a group reduces the social effectiveness of the group. There are other divisive influences, e.g. the middle-class idea of grown-up children living apart from their parents in the shared flat has now become wide-spread in upper working-class families, a son or daughter is often away at college—only about one-fifth of our university students live at home; modern individualised facilities for travel; the over-clinical nature of many new housing estates and new towns, etc.

To these, unfortunately all too often, must be added the influence of education. Once the docker's son becomes a scientist and climbs up from L.W.C. to H.M.C. relations at home may never be quite the same again. The common ground between father and son may shrink to a narrow area of reminiscence. The generation gap is much more often an education gap.

The groups centred around the churches meant much a generation ago. Many children grew up in the friendly, familiar, predictable congregation and its associated Sunday school, youth groups, etc. It was sometimes a place of enjoyment, sometimes of boredom but always somewhere to which one belonged—a refuge, a haven, solid, safe, known, permanent. But in recent years church life, with notable shining exceptions here and there, has shrunk to little more than the provision of opportunities for worship for those who want it. It is no longer the living hub of the district or village. The warm security it gave to previous generations has too often been replaced by an impersonal service. The worshipping community has often become a group of worshipping individuals.

At the same time as the socially integrative influence of the church has diminished the concept of the neighbourhood school, once almost universal, has been increasingly abandoned for economic, educational or, indeed, social reasons. In the village community the church or chapel and the school were the axes around which life revolved. Today the school may be closed and its children bussed daily to the local market town. In the towns larger school units are being created but often catering for irregular catchment areas contrived to produce a cross-section of all the social strata in the town. A typical county borough of a quarter of a million inhabitants may now concentrate the whole of its secondary school population into four or five large units, often sited on the periphery of the town. A few years ago there were probably twenty small secondary schools each the hub of its own locality, fostering a sense of community. The educational and social gains from the reorganisation are, of course, great, but the cohesion of the localities has suffered—and all our towns are, or were, groups of localities, almost villages, each with its own character, each one home to its people in a more intimate sense than the town itself could ever be.

Similar influences are at work in the other groups in which previous generations of children found security. The pioneering, camp-fire type of appeal of cubs, scouts, brownies and guides has waned in the age of technology. The young child's hours between school and bed are limited and children's youth movements have to compete for them against television. The youth-service clubs attract probably one-in-three of the 14–15 age group but their influence decreases rapidly above this age group, and, as 14 is the lower age limit it is almost non-existent below it. No matter where one looks, the groups in which children live and grow to maturity possess less cohesion than in the past. The old closely-knit matrices of warmth, affection and familiarity are giving way to looser groupings under the pressure of technological and societal change and our children are the losers. One wonders how much of the growth of juvenile delinquency is due to the consequent lack of security, warmth and affection. 'He who steals, steals love.'

Juveniles found guilty in Magistrates' Courts

1959	1969
98,372	118,724

The compensatory action by education can be of two kinds. First the school itself should be a community with all that that implies. Unfortunately some are not. A school which fails to develop the individual potential of its pupils is an inadequate community; a school which fails its deviant pupils is equally lacking. A school community should be a place where a child can '. . . grow in wisdom and in stature and in favour with God and man.'

It must be secure, physically secure in protecting the child from harm and emotionally secure in protecting him from injustice, fear and ridicule. It must be a compassionate community of caring members, motivated by real concern for each other and not by maudlin sentimentality. It must be a congenial community, not only free from strain but also lightened by happiness. It must be a vital community where there is the constant stimulation of successful effort, of creativity, of innovation, of approbation. It must be a place where each individual, no matter how modest his gifts, has his identity as a person affirmed and contributes it to the communal life.

This is the only kind of medium in which children can grow and, if growth be the purpose of education, it is the medium the schools must consciously set out to create. This was always their duty but in an age of looser, less cohesive sub-groups, the need is greater than ever before. Paradoxically, modern society with its technologically created affluence is squeezing security and affection out of the lives of our children. The schools must put them back.

A particular problem arises in the open secondary school which must be large enough to provide a sufficiently flexible organisation to cater for the full ability range and to produce an adequate sixth form. Sixth-form teaching skills are scarce and valuable and, for this reason alone, must be deployed sensibly. However, recent experience has to some extent revised earlier views on size and the five-form entry school now appears to be educationally defensible. It may well be that with the growth of sixth forms, the rationalising of the secondary-stage work of the further education colleges and the schools doing similar work, and the growth of educational technology, even smaller schools will be found to be viable.

It is only too easy for the very large school to develop an impersonal ethos, an atmosphere in which the efficiency of the organisation becomes an end in itself and the staff and pupils the raw material with which it is concerned. Of course, chaos must be prevented by efficient organisation but if the system becomes too obtrusive, too monolithic or too inflexible, the sense of community is stifled. In many schools considerable ingenuity is shown in creating sub-groups between the normal teaching groups and the school group in which the child, particularly those at the lower end of the age range, can know and be known. It is important that staffing standards should be generous enough to make this possible. It is equally important that the planning of large new schools should take account of this first-line division into sub-groups and that the education-factory concept should give way to rather cosy domestic blocks for them.

A striking example of the efforts being made by architects to combat the impersonal atmosphere is to be seen at the Clissold Park Comprehensive School in London where an ancient footpath known as Church Walk has been retained as a central feature in the

H

school and paved with bricks. This imports an element almost of domesticity into a new large school.

Having achieved this, it is important that the sub-groups do not become so self-contained and isolated that they destroy the overall cohesion of the school community. Shared, whole school activities, the very stuff of which school communities are built, are physically difficult in the 1000+ schools unless the architect has appreciated their importance and made provision for them. The secular school assembly at which the minutiae of school life are gathered up into their community context is of considerable importance in establishing a corporate identity—unless, of course, it is nothing more than the promulgation of new edicts or a general reading of the riot act by the headmaster.

A great deal more important, however, is the daily act of worship with which the secular assembly should not be confused—although it often is. Here, in shared worship, lies a major opportunity to create, sustain and deepen the sense of community. Often it falls far short of this objective. Where this occurs it is almost always because its form is in the mould which was universal a generation ago and this simply is not good enough today. There are perhaps one or two essentials. The most careful and thoughtful planning is necessary. A hurried search through the hymn and prayer books by the headmaster a few minutes before it starts is a certain recipe for miserable failure. Both the planning and the execution should involve more than the headmaster. After all it is community worship and both staff and pupils should be involved. While the content will usually be Christian in origin, although not always, it should, like religious education, be open and not aim at indoctrination, although clearly in most hymns and many prayers assumptions are necessarily made. Above all it should be relevant to the world in which the children live—a world which includes a great many people of other faiths, a world with many problems and many opportunities. In a society where increasing numbers of people are communally deprived how foolish we should be to abandon this feature in our schools.

Whilst the assumptions which give rise to the very large school should be constantly under review it is equally important at the other end of the scale to question those which are used to justify the closure of the majority of village schools. Progressive approaches to curriculum and teaching methods have made the village primary school a much more attractive educational proposition than was believed even ten years ago, provided, of course, its buildings can be made adequate. It is also, with its teacher-pupil intimacy, its open fire, its familiar playing space, as near to the atmosphere of the home as it is possible to get. Unless there are quite peculiar local circumstances the removal of young children at the infant stage from a school of this kind to a bigger unit some miles away cannot be justified on educational grounds. It is flying in the face of all we know about the needs of young children to suggest that it can. At the 7-11 stage there may sometimes be a case, though here also the educational grounds put forward by the local education authority to justify closure are also frequently open to great doubt.

This leaves the economic case for concentrating rural children in area schools and, whilst it is a consideration which cannot be ignored in view of the pressure to find the resources for education, it should be clearly recognised that the issue to be decided is usually economy *v*. educational advantage. One wonders how much longer rural communities will be prepared to allow their children to lose their cosy, secure, socially and educationally attractive schools in order to reduce the rate poundage by a few coppers—especially in an age when their warmth and security have never been needed more.

Thus both local education authorities in the type of schools they provide and the teachers in the school organisation they devise, can do much to create the community life which is necessary to meet the basic social needs of children without which they cannot achieve their potential development. But there is another way in which education can make a major contribution not only to meeting these needs but also to enriching communal life outside the school. The basis of community is communication in its broadest sense of social responsibility, i.e. identifying with the lives, problems and needs of others. The school community itself will give many opportunities for the growth and practice of social obligation, but no matter how much care is taken to create a sense of community the school must inevitably be a limited community with a narrow range of possibilities for service to others, e.g. it has no old people or sick, among whom so many of the problems of modern society are to be found. If the range of social obligation is extended to other schools in the neighbourhood a wider area of problem, and therefore of opportunity, may often be found, e.g. a special school for spina bifida children in Sheffield has a good deal of its equipment devised and made in the local comprehensive school. Similarly, an infant school in Newcastle upon Tyne has much of its wooden and metal equipment made in the craft classes in a nearby comprehensive school.

However, even with this extremely useful co-operation, the range of opportunity is limited. But outside the school, surrounding it on every side, is another community teeming with problems large and small calling out for service, care and compassion at every turn. If the creation of a highly sensitive sense of social obligation is an educational objective, and it surely must be one of the more important, it would be just as foolish to ignore the vast opportunities for service in the community outside the school, or group of schools, as it would be for the teacher of reading to ignore the newspapers. And the benefits would not all lie in the relevance it brought into the school. Social service in the world outside the school would be an integrating influence—the activities like strands running out from the school-hub pulling the neighbourhood together. Anything which forges links between the school and the community it serves is to be welcomed.

The connections between community service and religious and moral training are obvious enough—though perhaps the majority of schools still ignore them. How much more valuable it would be for a group of secondary-stage children to paint a lonely, aged pensioner's kitchen than to sit through an arid lesson in theology! But the relevance it can give to other areas of the curriculum is equally valuable. The Schools Council Working Paper No. 17 (H.M.S.O., 1968) makes extremely useful suggestions for the development of a community-service programme as a regular part of the curriculum. There is no reason why service of this kind should be confined to older pupils. There are many opportunities for the very youngest children in the infant school to undertake simple services for others. In the Working Paper referred to above, Dr. Miller, the Birmingham Medical Officer of Health, is quoted as saying that no child is so young that he cannot help another. Nor is it an activity to be limited to the 'Newsom' child. A sense of social responsibility is just as important to the more able, perhaps more so. Selflessness and humility come less easily to the more able.

Young people themselves, by their own initiative, have in the Young Volunteer Force, V.S.O. and a host of other bodies, become massively involved in community service in recent years. In so doing they have often shamed their schools for their neglect of its possibilities in education.

What better way of drawing out the potential for good in a young person than encouraging him to undertake clear and definite service for others? The technology-dominated world in which he will live his adult life will be harsh enough. If he is to survive in it as a person he will require values which transcend the selfish pursuit of affluence and material well-being.

The school can foster the growth of these values and the concept of service must be central to them but school life is short, no more than the law requires for almost half of our young people. For most people the two most formative periods of life fall just outside each end of the statutory school life—the earliest years and the middle teens. Between the end of school life and the great watershed of marriage at about 22 years for women and 24 years for men with all the sharing and selflessness for which it calls, there is a hiatus of, on average, eight years when the idealism of school days can run into the ground like a stream in the desert. This may be as true for the school leavers going into higher or further education as for those who go straight into employment.

This blind spot in our educational provision must receive much more attention as the education service is developed if the influence of the schools is not largely to be wasted. This applies to the intellectual side of education but it applies equally to the growth of a sense of

social responsibility and, indeed, to the whole field of moral education. Eventually society will find the will and the resources to extend
formal education to the end of the turbulent formative years and not
cut it off in mid-stream as now. Until it does so a great deal of
educational effort is wasted. The pot is too often taken from the kiln
too soon. That is why it is often half-baked and brittle—why it often
lacks lustre.

Until society awakens to the fact that it is only half educating
half of its youth—if that is not a contradiction in terms—we must
make greater efforts to help school leavers to keep alive the few
glowing embers kindled in school—a desire to learn, a sense of
wonder, a love of reading and perhaps of creating beauteous things,
an interest in current affairs, the love of truth, the touch-stone of
reason, objectivity, compassion—above all compassion and all it
entails. At the moment the youth service touches no more than
29 per cent of young people, in spite of the dedicated work of
thousands of youth workers, and most of the membership falls
away after 16 or 17. The bulk of the membership is at the 14–15 age
groups, i.e. among those still at school. The membership of girls is
lower than of boys and they fall away at an even earlier age probably
mainly because of their earlier maturity but also because the vast
majority of youth workers are males who find difficulty in creating a
service which appeals to the 16+ girl. The voluntary organisations,
however, attract a higher proportion of all ages than the youth
service proper. The meagreness of this effort, scarcely meriting the
name 'service,' is deplorable. Not only is the size of the service
ridiculously inadequate but the above figures do indicate that it is
rapidly losing its relevance to the needs of the modern teenager.
The authorities appear to be quite unaware of its utter inadequacy.

Following a proposal by the Albermarle Committee, an advisory
body, the Youth Service Development Council, was established to
advise on the service in England and Wales. Now, a decade after
Albermarle, the Council has completed a thorough study which has
been published under the title of *Youth and the Community in the 70's*
(H.M.S.O.). As its name implies the central concept is of a new
service not restricted to the 14–20 age band, contacting young

people wherever they are found, embedded in dual-purpose schools and voluntary organisations at the lower ages and recognising the adult status of the upper ages. Such a service could bridge the gulfs which at present often separate school, industry, trade unions and social services. Its aim would be to enable young people to find their place in society rather than to provide introverted clubs for the few. It has, of course, considerable implications for the organisation of the service, the training of workers, allocation of resources, the nature of youth activities, etc.

Unfortunately the Government rejected the report in a Parliamentary reply on 29th March 1971, but there is no reason why local authorities, voluntary organisations and training agencies as well as industry, commerce and trade unions should not use it to guide the development of youth work in the 70's. It could do much to provide the congenial social context which the young child needs and to involve the post-school teenager in the life of the community before he acquires family responsibilities and his social-cultural education comes to maturity. These are vulnerable years in which lack of community, lack of security, lack of involvement can do irreparable harm.

Intertwined with the problem of creating, preserving and deepening community life is the related problem of the use of leisure. Education has for many years recognised the existence of the problem, accepted some responsibility and then done little about it. Examination papers in education show almost identical questions on education for the use of leisure set regularly over the past forty years. It has been regarded more as an academic theme for discussion than an urgent educational problem. Few teachers or administrators have made it a major objective.

Yet if the purpose of education is to enable people to lead happy lives, satisfying both to themselves and to those among whom they live, it cannot ignore this growing part of them. The wealthier members of society always had a fair amount of leisure and their own independent education system taught them to play games competently and to acquire graces which would enable them to enjoy it. But today the manual worker probably has as much leisure as the professional worker or business executive. The bargaining power of the trade unions is used as much to shorten working hours and to increase paid holidays as to increase pay. But the response of education has not matched their success. Here again an inherently conservative service insists on its pre-response time-lag.

In 1951 only 35 per cent of the labour force were entitled to two weeks' paid holiday; in 1971 the comparable figure is 94 per cent and of these 34 per cent have between two and three weeks. Similarly with working hours, in 1951 agreed weekly hours were between 42 and 45 and in 1971 between 40 and 42 (*Britain Today*, H.M.S.O., and *Britain 1950–51*, H.M.S.O.).

In the face of the trend disclosed by figures such as these it would make sense if the vocational bias which has emerged in the curriculum in the past two decades, and which is now increasingly irrelevant (see Chapter 2) gave way to a leisure bias. The quality of a person's leisure probably has a greater bearing on the quality of his total living than his hours at work. Technological development is providing time and money to use in pursuits other than providing the basic needs of food, shelter and clothing.

How, then, can education translate its long-held academic interest in leisure into a major educational objective? Perhaps it is important first to be quite clear about how it cannot do so. Education for leisure almost always brings to the mind of the teacher visions of basket-work, bee-keeping, woodwork, stamp-collecting, etc.—interesting hobbies in the teacher's opinion. Of course, activities of this kind provide absorbing interests for many people but when they do so they are very largely the product of an attitude of mind which is essential to the satisfying use of leisure. It is partly an attitude towards learning—liking to learn and knowing how to learn—but it is also much more. It is an uncynical attitude of mind which refuses to be bored. It unashamedly preserves into adult life a sense of wonder, the greatest glory of the very young child, a curiosity about the world and all its mysteries, about man and all his mysteries, a compelling desire to explore by seeing, hearing, reading, acting, doing—by creating. But how often this wondrousness in man is killed stone-cold dead in early childhood by the cynical parent ('Don't waste your time on that nonsense—get on with your homework!') or the uninspired teacher who covers a piece of creative writing with red ink or who tries to 'teach' seven-years-olds to draw. It is only too easy, of course, for the questionning of the modern child to degenerate into scepticism. It is the school's task to see not only that it does not do so but that it is sublimated into awareness and sensitivity. If teachers can create this attitude, or preserve it, they need not worry their heads about useful hobbies and crafts. The adult whose schooling has not torn away the 'trailing clouds of glory' will never lack hobbies and interests. On the other hand the bored adult will get nothing out of them no matter how excellently he may be able to make dovetail joints, wrought iron weather vanes or recognise the redbreasted merganser. Paradoxically, to get the most out of his living in the age of technology, modern man must retain an almost primitive humility and spontaneity. He must not be afraid to stand and stare at the sunset, the gigantic power station or the simple flower—unashamedly lost in wonder.

Education can raise the quality of life in modern society by preserving this sensitivity, not only unimpaired but deepened and enhanced. If it does so there will be few problems about the use of leisure in adult life.

But, given the desire to undertake satisfying leisure activities, it is important that local education authorities should take much more seriously the duty laid on them in Section 41 of the Education Act, 1944 to provide facilities for '. . . leisure time occupation . . . cultural training and recreative activities . . . for any persons over compulsory school age who are able and willing to profit by the facilities.'

A modest programme of non-vocational classes in the winter months, useful as they may be, is scarcely sufficient to discharge this clear duty. An example, indeed almost a prototype, of what can be done if public goodwill and interest are mobilised, is to be seen at the Midlands Art Centre at Birmingham where 17,500 children from 245 schools are enrolled as members at the same time as a family membership of 6000. An average of 5000 people a week are regularly involved in a wide range of activities in a purpose-built

centre with high quality of design and accommodation, on which
£¾ m. has been invested in building and equipment. The Centre is
owned and run by the Cannon Hill Trust. Capital investment has
been shared by three partners—central government, local government, and private donors. The private sector had provided
£385,000 up to 1970. For the triennium 1970–3 the continuing
investment programme calls for a contribution from each partner of
over £¼ m.

The whole centre is being created on a beautiful site in a Birmingham Park. Its services include such facilities as an excellent library,
exhibitions, evening courses (at least 30 at any one time over a
twelve-month period), weekend family sessions, squash courts,
junior arts club with pottery, woodwork, painting, sculpture, drama,
music, photography, etc. It is also unique in having the Resident
Midlands Arts Theatre Company—its largest single service to the
public. In 1969/70 the company staged 12 plays and gave 523
performances. 'In the area of cultural activity the keynote is desir-
ability, creativity, exploration, non-conformity, independence.
This does not mean indiscipline or anarchy, but it does imply . . .
self choice, self-application, self-direction, self-discipline.' (A
Survey for Unesco, 1969, by Alicia Randle and John English—Mr.
English is now the director of the Midlands Arts Centre.)

The importance of community, discussed in the first part of this
chapter, is extremely relevant to the use of leisure. A person who
feels he is not ' . . . an Iland intire unto itselfe' will seek out his
fellow men and become involved with them in shared activities.
Many people find in community service opportunities which absorb
all their leisure and give tremendous purpose to their lives, e.g.
the playgroup, the over sixty club, Oxfam, hospital visits, etc. But
there is a wider sense in which the two are related. Almost all leisure
activities for which local education authorities provide facilities
involve groups of individuals working together. This adds to the
enjoyment of them and at the same time reinforces the sense of
community. The sharing of an activity has much more reality in
such a context as the Midlands Arts Centre than in the uncomfortable desks of a school classroom in the typical non-vocational

evening class. Sharing involves more than 20 ladies doing pottery painting in the same room at the same time, e.g. it means discussing with each other materials, design, techniques, etc., so that the creation, whether it be a hat, a pot, a dress, a picture or a coffee table is the product of co-operation—of communion.

In a very real sense social responsibility and the satisfying use of leisure are closely related—a fact of which government, local authorities and teachers should never lose sight.

8

Communication

The ability of human beings to communicate information, ideas or feelings to their fellows, rapidly, accurately and fluently, has always been a primary factor in man's evolution. Today, when the technology he has created is outpacing his social evolution, it is the skill in greatest need of improvement. There are three broad reasons for this. First, the sheer mechanics of state, industry, commerce, leisure use and society demand the instantaneous communication of data and ideas; second, one of the major ills of our society is the loss of a sense of community which can only be arrested by improved communication between people and the sub-groups in which they live; and, third, it is the major educational skill upon which all learning and growth of personality depend.

One of the more obvious aspects of the state's activity is its increasing tendency to intervene in industry, commerce and the private lives of its citizens. One administration may be marginally more, or less, interventionist than another but the trend is never halted. Industry, science, technology, economics and society itself are becoming increasingly complicated and demand a growing degree of central direction. *Laissez-faire* today could only result in chaos. All advanced nations now accept national economic planning varying from the comprehensive planning of the communist states, through the mixed economy of Britain to the use of fiscal and credit controls in the U.S.A.

Side by side with the growth of economic planning most countries have erected social-security systems which also vary from the British or Swedish welfare states to the stop-gap arrangements in some other countries. Both developments have involved massive interventionist national policies.

Added to this, the growth of technology has inevitably led to greater government control. The motor-car would destroy us without laws to regulate its use. Our factories and mines would be highly unsafe without regulations laying down working conditions and rules governing the use of machinery. The most alert housewife would be duped constantly without legislation about the sale of goods and the purity of foods. Lake Ullswater, from time immemorial free to all users, now has highly restrictive bye-laws because of the activities of water-skiers.

All this vast machinery regulating our lives is the product of a huge but inevitable bureaucracy. Of course, bureaucracy is not inherently wicked or oppressive. It may indeed be wholly beneficient but whether it is or not depends to a very great extent on the degree of literacy among the people whom it serves, on their ability to read (especially the small print!), to write (the critical letter to the press, the intelligent query to H.M.I. of T., etc.) and, above all, to comprehend the rules and regulations. A highly literate people will demand, and get, a sensitive bureaucracy, and this is the only condition under which it is tolerable in a democratic state. 'Your obedient servant' ought to mean what it says but it will only do so if the recipient of the letter, as well as the sender, understands it. Literacy can make the world safe for bureaucracy.

The growth of larger industrial units has been referred to in Chapters 2 and 5. The greater remoteness of policy making which follows from it is usually mitigated to some extent by more efficient management structures. Nevertheless, effective management depends upon effective communication all the way down the line, from the boardroom to the work bench. The need is all the greater because of the growing strength of labour and its willingness to assert it. A steady stream of information not only about decisions affecting conditions of employment, but about the company, its policies, finances, progress and prospects—readily given, readily understood—would do much to prevent industrial unrest and improve efficiency. Nor should it be a one-way process. Management and workers should be equally attentive to each other. Indeed we have reached a point in industrial relations where a permanent dialogue is essential.

But given a willingness on the part of one side to supply views or information, the effectiveness of their dissemination depends upon the lucidity with which they are expressed and the ability to read or listen and comprehend on the part of those at whom they are aimed.

Within the trade unions themselves there is the same need for more meaningful communication between officials, shop-stewards and the rank-and-file. If the unions are to remain true to their democratic ideals, and they were the very cradle of modern British democracy, they must not allow 'Brother' to degenerate into 'Big Brother.' This also demands a permanent dialogue—a sharing of ideas. But ideas cannot be shared unless they can be expressed coherently, taken on board, examined critically and answered objectively.

Perhaps the most obvious need for better communication—simply in order to survive with a reasonable degree of comfort in the late twentieth-century world—is one of the more important. Technology has made a dramatic impact on our lives in recent years. Highly efficient machines have taken the drudgery out of domestic work and largely out of industry, transportation has become individualised, speedy and efficient. Entertainment is more sophisticated and, more often than not, provided for the masses; communication with the ends of the earth is almost instantaneous. But the revolution in our material lives, like the revolution in the activities of the state, demands the thorough understanding of an unending stream of instructions which are often couched in highly specialised terms. Mrs. Smith must be able to read and understand the instructions with her new deep freeze or on the newly marketed washing powder packet. Mr. Smith should be able to follow the manual provided with his new car or the small print on the packet of rose fertiliser. John Smith must be familiar with the makers' instructions on the use of his hi-fi equipment or his tape recorder. Mary Smith clearly cannot make the new dress advertised in *Woman* unless she can follow the instructions and the pattern. At every turn modern living demands the ability to read accurately and with understanding, for the misunderstanding of a single word could lead to a minor disaster in any of the above examples, e.g. if young John connected the three wires to the wrong terminals in the plug of his equipment the consequences could be extremely serious. The whole vast field of instructions, explanatory booklets and manuals, etc., thrown up in our technological society is a goldmine of material for practice in reading and comprehension. How much more useful and interesting to use it than a great deal of the uninspiring and motivationally negative reading material which our children have to endure. Children learn when they have a convincing motive to do so. The assertion by the teacher that reading is a useful skill in adult life is not a motive; the desire to know how a car engine works or how to make a dress is a very effective one. If the goal stands out clear and desirable most children will cheerfully scale the foothills of reading in order to reach it. The trouble is that so often they can see nothing beyond the foothills!

In Chapter 2 the probable need to retrain and acquire new specialisms on a number of occasions in a working life was mentioned. This too will require a higher degree of literacy in the future. Retraining of adults must necessarily be different from the more leisurely initial training where practice will be more important than precept. At the age of 40 or 50 there is not the time for this. A great deal more will depend upon the spoken and written word and their effectiveness will be determined by the efficiency of both poles of the process—lucidity of expression and accuracy of comprehension. Thus a higher standard of literacy as well as of education generally are very relevant to creating an economy which is flexible and responsive to changing demand for our products.

The health of the economy also necessarily demands close and constant relations with other countries, most of whom have different languages, particularly our nearest neighbours in Europe. The urgent need for improving both the quality and extent of language teaching is discussed in Chapter 9. Our traditional national neglect of languages other than our own may be a legacy of imperial pretensions or of our age-old insularity. But, today, dependent as we are on trade for our living, it is an unforgivable example of national laziness. In the close-knit modern world the term "illiterate" is extending to include those of us who have no proficiency in any language other than our own.

Evidence to support the central place of the power to communicate among educational objectives is almost limitless. The mechanics of our world depend upon it at every turn. For this reason, if for no other, it lies at the heart of all education from the nursery school to the university and beyond.

But there are other reasons. It is the life blood of community, the bond which integrates individual members of a family or a trade union or a church into a single entity with a life of its own. It creates one-ness out of diversity. A similar theme is found in the Christian story and ethic. The crucifixion is spoken of as the at-one-ment. Through it, the body of Christ gathered up into itself all the members of His church and it is celebrated in the communion service. The equation of one-ness and communion. The theme is familiar enough in the smaller sub-groups in which we live but less so when considered in relation to social class which was discussed in Chapter 6. Any impediment to communication, whether it is the barriers of class, language, wealth, vocation or any other, detracts from oneness and, therefore, from all the benefits of security, strength of purpose, efficiency, etc., which can flow from it. The ability and desire to speak to and understand the other man is the one essential ingredient of every community.

Finally, it is not only necessary to the mechanics of our world and the creation of true community but without the ability to read, write and comprehend the written and spoken word, the learning process would be retarded. And cumulatively so, for there is a constantly growing discrepancy between actual progress made by a child and his potential if, on the way, an essential step or skill has not been mastered. And the ability to read is a collection of sub-skills. Ausubel called this the cumulative deficits hypothesis. If some aspect of Johnny's reading or writing has been omitted or overstressed, for this is equally harmful, the detriment he will suffer over the whole range of school activity will grow bigger each year.

Of course the importance of reading and writing has always been understood by teachers but, unfortunately, because of this, they elevated them into ends in themselves and the 3 R's became an unholy trinity around which the lesser 'subjects' such as music, history, science, art, etc., were fitted in if time could be found for them. In all the old time-tables (and some present ones) they occupied pride of place, the child's peak learning period each day. Entry into the grammar school depended upon proficiency in them. Reluctant children were literally forced to acquire skills but they had little opportunity to use them except in school exercises painfully contrived to improve them. 'Learning to read,' i.e. merely decoding words, became an end in itself, a school exercise like adding 695 and 234 or dividing £14 2s. 7d. by 4, unrelated to the reality of the child's everyday life.

It was because of the prevalent excessive skill training at the expense of education that the Hadow Report (1931) suggested child-centred education but formal training in the necessary skills. This dichotomy has also its more recent advocates among whom D. H. Parker has developed his views with great thoroughness in *Schooling for Individual Excellence* (Nelson, 1963). This approach has two drawbacks. It is extremely difficult to import the relevance of a real-life situation into formal training but unless it can be given meaning in this way its success will not be great. Secondly, the transfer from formal reading to child-centred activity is notoriously difficult, as is any transfer of formal training. Those of us who learnt French or German as isolated skills by formal methods will remember with anguish the difficulty we encountered in trying to use them on the continent.

There is some evidence that Johnny is not learning to read adequately in the sense that reading involves more than the mere de-coding of words, however efficiently he may be able to do that, but also involves immediate and complete understanding of their meaning. Dr. Joyce Morris in her book *Standards and Progress in*

I

Reading (N.F.E.R., 1966) found that 10–14 per cent of 15-year-old children were poor readers. Two years later Keith Gardner of Nottingham Institute of Education went further and claimed that he could not find any evidence of a rise in standards of literacy for thirty years, if literacy meant understanding and the ability to evaluate and criticise the printed word as well as to decode it. In the same year Dr. Morris in *The Teaching of Reading* (Ward Lock, 1968) pointed out that low reading standards were not only a problem for the schools but that the more complex reading skills required at university level were equally deficient.

On the other hand the Department of Education and Science is satisfied that standards '. . . have risen considerably since 1948 when the first of a series of periodical surveys was carried out. This is true of both eleven-year-olds and fifteen year-olds.' (*Reports on Education*, H.M.S.O., July 1970, No. 64.) The results of national samples are given in *Progress in Reading 1948–64* (H.M.S.O.) and of local samples in *Standards and Progress in Reading* by J. M. Morris (N.F.E.R., 1966).

Bruce Kemble, an education correspondent who has made reading standards his special interest, has criticised this assessment on two grounds—that national survey figures at best merely show that we have made up the reverse in standards suffered during the second world war and that they are not concerned with reading in its complete sense of involving a high degree of comprehension as well as mechanical skill (*Give Your Child a Chance* (The Garden City Press, 1970) and articles in the *Daily Express*).

Whatever the truth between these two views may be, it must be conceded that there is evidence of a weight and respectability which cannot be entirely ignored, that reading standards give some cause for disquiet at a time when society demands considerably higher standards. And it may well be that the divorce of mechanical skill-acquiring from skill-using in real-life situations is a major cause. Reading in school must be much more than the recognition of words. It must also involve a high degree of comprehension including the ability to evaluate and criticise the content. When it falls short of this objective Johnny, in the present-day context, has not learnt to read. It and its twin skill of writing, together with the ability to reason (see Chapter 5), are by far the most important skills the child can acquire at school.

It is not the purpose of this chapter to tell teachers how to teach reading. Teaching methods are a complex of human relationships and every teacher must work them out for himself. However, from the more successful methods currently in use it is possible to distil two common factors. First, in view of the long-recognised problem of the transfer of formal training it surely makes sense to abandon the confusing, unreal dichotomy altogether and develop the skills of both reading and writing as and when they are needed by the child himself in his own activities. This approach demands great patience from both parent and teacher. They must not lose their nerve when progress seems delayed or patchy but should remember that the ultimate gain more than compensates for the initial worry as the fifth, sixth or even seventh birthday passes before the spark really ignites. The motivation to read should not be remote from the child but should be within his own experience. The 'Reader' was for generations a factor in low reading standards. Its content and language were far too often alien to the child's experience. To him reading, writing, painting, modelling, music and drama should all be skills with which he can express ideas, information and feelings with joy, creativity and accuracy. The child himself should look upon all these media as one genus, different ways in which he can record and transmit himself to others and not as dreary skills demanded by the adult world as part of the initiation rites into it. They should be means by which he can both establish his identity as a person and his one-ness with his fellows.

Secondly, when success and the confidence it generates are of such key importance to progress it does seem sensible to limit or remove the major hurdle of irregularities of pronunciation in our language. Imagine the problems presented to a young child by such words as through, bough, cough and dough or, our and colour or, also and pal or, to and top, or some and home, etc. It was to remove this impediment and regularise the relationship between symbol and sound that Sir James Pitman developed the initial teaching alphabet (i.t.a.). To do this 24 letters of the existing alphabet were retained and to these were added 20 new symbols. The new 44-symbol alphabet enabled different sounds to be represented logically with a one-to-one relationship between spoken sound and written symbol. It also had the great merit that older methods of teaching could be pursued in the medium of the new alphabet.

Wuns upon a tiem ſhær woſ a toi mæker caulld doctor coppælius, hœ mæd ſhe mœst buetifœl toiſ. hee cœd mæk dollſ ſhat waukt and lœkt very, very liefliek.

Example of i.t.a.

i.t.a. has quickly, and rightly, caught the imagination of teachers throughout the country. By June 1966 1554 infant schools in England and Wales were using it and there is a considerable and growing range of published teaching material available. In 1966 the Schools Council initiated a major enquiry under Professor F. W. Warburton and Vera Southgate into its use and value as a teaching medium. Their findings were published in *i.t.a.—an independent evaluation* (John Murray/W. & R. Chambers, 1969) and are best summarised in the following quotations—

'In the vast majority of cases, infant headteachers and class teachers who had used i.t.a. were favourably impressed. Some of their comments denoted approval which amounted to the utmost fervour' (page 35).

'The general conclusion drawn from these various researches is that i.t.a. is a superior medium to t.o. in teaching young children to read' (page 275).

'Both the verbal evidence and the research indicate that in the majority of schools, although not in all, infants using i.t.a. have learned to read earlier, more easily and at a faster rate than similar children using t.o.' (pages 282-3).

In view of the quite remarkable success being achieved with i.t.a. in the early stages of reading, and after all it is this stage which is all important, it is difficult to understand why its use has not become universal.

Many teachers without experience of it are deterred by the thought of the return to the standard alphabet which must be made once facility in reading is acquired. They regard it as being almost as difficult and incomprehensible as Apollo's return from the moon. In practice, however, it appears to occur quite naturally and presents little or no difficulty. The point which is forgotten by those who stress this problem is that, by then, the child can read with ease, confidence and enjoyment. Given this kind of ability, re-entry into t.o. is taken in its stride.

There are, of course, other media which eliminate the irregularities of pronunciation—some involving colours representing different sounds and, of course, the International Phonetic Alphabet. None, however, appears to have achieved the success of i.t.a.

Thus, whatever methods are used to enable children to acquire this all-important skill there does appear to be a case for ending the rigid division between skill-acquiring and skill-using and also for the use of a medium which eliminates irregularities of pronunciation in the initial stages until confidence has been built up.

As the child progresses through the school there is increasing need for reading speed. Speed reading techniques should find a place in the upper forms of the secondary school. Civilised living demands an enormous amount of reading, very often in strictly limited time, and the schools are not doing nearly sufficient to develop this speed. The techniques have been developed with considerable success in recent years but almost exclusively with adults—very often business executives. But there is now an urgent need to apply them in schools, for the ability to read rapidly is a considerable asset to almost everyone in the modern world.

Equally important is the need for growing comprehension of increasingly difficult material. H.M.I. Mr. Gilbert Peaker estimated that nine out of ten 11-year-olds could not read a *Times* editorial, and one out of ten could not read the *Daily Mirror*. If these figures are accurate they should give cause for concern. The explanation of them may well be, as in the case of the conflicting evidence over reading standards generally, the failure to transfer the ability to read 'school' material to the challenges of the outside world. If this is the case it reinforces the plea made elsewhere in this book for a much greater use of material trawled from the everyday life of a typical family, in particular the press. This printed matter, newspapers, forms, brochures, instruction leaflets, election material, advertising material, etc., is available in vast quantities, free of charge. It is infinitely more valuable teaching material than a good deal of the carefully contrived, expertly and expensively produced, publications which are a feature of our schools.

Reading is the primary skill with which education is concerned but the ability to convert language into written symbols is also important. The modern world has only two requirements. First, as in reading, speed is almost all-important. It is in fact so important that typing should find a place for all pupils at the secondary stage. In the world of business and commerce the typewriter is used a good deal more than the pen but it is becoming a tool in general use also. *The Observer* has a special offer to readers each week and among the grillers, barbecue sets, rocking chairs, etc., the portable typewriter has found its place. Before long no home will be without one and we should now see that all older children become proficient in its use. How sensible it would be if 'O' and 'A' level papers were typed— and how much easier for the examiners!

The second requirement is legibility. It is not much use writing rapidly if no one else can read it! But provided there is speed and legibility the style is quite unimportant and no child or student ought to be demoralised or penalised and have his spontaneity destroyed because his handwriting does not conform to some preconceived notion of style or neatness. There is little doubt that character can show itself in handwriting. To try to prevent its doing so would be a pity. Channels of expression available to human beings are few enough, and it might actually be harmful to personality to do so.

Both reading and writing are closely bound up in their development with spoken language. Poverty or richness of language are a product of the child's experience and the home and school provide by far the greater part of this. The Plowden Report pointed out that 29 per cent of all homes in this country have five books or less. Equally deficient is the conversation between many parents and their children—deficient in ideas, vocabulary and sympathy. Largely because of these differences some children will be able to read fluently before they come to school; others, of equal ability, will not be able to read at 8 years.

But, in present-day society, linguistic deprivation may occur from quite other causes in middle-class homes. Whole families have become addicted to television and where this has occurred conversation is frowned upon. 'There is some evidence that television inhibits conversation. Fine speaks of "unity without conversation." Eleanor Maccoby feels that there is little interaction in a family watching television and that the increased contact (i.e. members of the family staying at home more to watch it) is not social. . . . Belson . . . found that the discussion of family affairs was reduced or displaced and that parental absorption often cut down on the normal parent-child exchanges.' (J. D. Halloran, *The Effects of Mass Communication*, Leicester University Press, 1965.)

The working mother has become the rule rather than the exception. Children are either deprived of her company because she is at her work or because she has to spend the evening doing her household chores which in a previous generation were always done when the children were at school. The development of new housing estates many miles from the town centres has created a generation of commuting fathers—often leaving home early and returning late.

All these changes are depriving children of the company and conversation of their parents. Because of them, as well as the all too familiar home where there is acute linguistic poverty anyhow, the schools must compensate by providing richness and variety of language experience. The need for this is greater than ever before. As part of this compensatory effort perhaps we can rid ourselves for ever of the ridiculous notion that school ought to be as silent as the tomb. It should be a place of unending conversation. The silent school is a thoroughly unwholesome, unnatural place subjecting young children to a mild form of torture and also failing in its duty to provide a language-rich environment.

Clearly, good speech is an essential skill in the modern world. It is important for specific purposes such as using the telephone or tape-recorder, and these ought to feature in school from the earliest age, but also for normal social intercourse. There is a high degree of mobility of labour today and this will certainly increase. George Smith of Tyneside must be understood in Birmingham, or in the board room if he moves vertically instead of horizontally. One would have expected this greater mobility, together with the influence of radio and television, to iron out local accents but, paradoxically, this has not happened. On the contrary, they have become respectable and are retained and used with pride! A generation ago a Scottish accent was the only socially acceptable deviant from standard English. Today we have no standard English pronunciaton—or even B.B.C. English! The present Prime Minister has a regional accent as had his immediate predecessor. The Beatles and Cilla Black have brought the Liverpool sound in from the provincial cold. Almost any accent is acceptable provided it is enunciated clearly, spoken without self-consciousness and, of course, couched in accurate grammar. This assertion of regionalism in language is a thoroughly wholesome and desirable reaction against the pressure for uniformity, and it has at last freed us from the snobbery and tyranny of the 'correct' accent. It is part and parcel of the movement to re-establish regional identity seen in Scottish and Welsh nationalism, the Maud proposals for local government, regional planning boards, etc. The weight of the schools in the past has been placed firmly on the side of the steam roller of uniformity, but this is no longer acceptable. There is no earthly reason why the boy from Liverpool or Newcastle should be forced to become bi-lingual. He should be encouraged to retain his regional accent and the school should help him to speak it with grace, enjoyment and pride.

What has been said about reading, writing and speech can be summarised by saying that modern living demands that the boundaries of literacy are pushed back beyond where they were a generation ago. Education fails its children today if they achieve nothing more than superficially efficient mechanical skill in them. The objective now is uninhibited fluency and creativity in the use of language and depth in the understanding of it.

But communication is wider than the use of language. Human beings reach out towards each other from their individual isolation to create community in other media. Music and the visual arts are the records of valuable feelings which can evoke equally valuable responses in others. The artist may create in order to communicate or merely to record his feelings but in either case he is expressing something in him for which words are an inadequate medium.

The human being lives on a number of levels—physical, intellectual, emotional, spiritual. To become fully himself and get the most out of his living, and to enable him to do so is the purpose of education, he must live, grow and fulfil himself on all these levels. Some people, unfortunately, scarcely leave the first. A great many never get beyond the second, but education must also concern itself with what lies beyond.

Insensitivity, where it exists in adults, is an indictment of the education system. Human beings require a finer awareness of and feeling for design, colour, form and the finer expressions of feeling by other people. And the other side to sensitivity is the ability to express one's own finer, deeper and more valuable feelings— in words certainly, but also in ways which do not have inherent in them the limitations of vocabulary and grammar.

Speech is often quite inadequate to express and communicate something in us which we feel worthy of expression. Words when expressed in the form of poetry are a more sensitive medium and when clothed in music they may enable even deeper feelings to be expressed. But however ordered or clothed, there may be depths in human beings which cannot use them—even in the most articulate of us. Colour and form may often carry the power to express further into the deeper and less accessible layers of man's mystery.

The great religions of the world discovered this long ago. The waning of religious belief and the falling off in religious observance throws a greater responsibility on the schools. Religious worship with its music, colour and ritual was for long a medium for the expression of emotion. With its decline other media are needed. But the search for Beauty may be no less rewarding in poetry, music and the visual arts than in worship—indeed they have much in common.

For many there will still be an un-expressible residue which neither poet nor musician, actor nor artist can reach. This is not the human tragedy; it is much more the human quest—to search throughout life for a Holy Grail. We may never find it, but the questing will give our lives purpose, meaning and satisfaction. And the beginning of the life-long quest to express and communicate is in youth—in the home and the school.

9

The Contracting World

Times taken by scheduled flights from London Airport—
To:

Newcastle	40 Minutes
Paris	1 hour
Rome	2 hours
Tel Aviv	4½ hours
New York	7½ hours
Cape Town	17 hours
Tokyo	14 hours

Item from a newspaper on 3rd May 1971—

'Today the Queen left for British Columbia. Her flight will take 10 hours. A century ago the same journey took the pioneers 10 months.'

At the turn of the century the size of the world depended upon one's bank balance. To the rich it was not very big. To the poor the oceans were almost unbridgeable. Today for the well-to-do jet travel has shrunk it to the size of Britain in 1900 and to the size of Europe for the less well off. Technology has enormously increased the speed and ease of travel and it has created the wealth for a very much wider social range to use it. Immigration to Canada was almost regarded as the final separation this side of eternity by working-class families only half a century ago. Today large numbers of people travel there by charter flights for holidays. Package holidays move farther afield each year. Spain was virtually unknown to all but the well-to-do at the end of the second world war. Today over 2,500,000 Britons spend their holidays there annually. Package holidays in East Africa and the Caribbean are now being offered in increasing numbers. Mombasa and the coast of Kenya will probably be as popular as the Costa Brava is today when the present primary-school children take their children on holiday.

Equally dramatic improvements in telecommunications have given us almost instant communication with every civilised corner of the globe. Submarine cables, constructed from new materials and almost indestructible, circle the globe and are now massively complemented by short-wave radio using 4 stationary (relative to earth) communications satellites—each one carrying a large number of simultaneous telephone conversations. International dialling is developing rapidly and the ordinary household subscriber in Britain can already in 1971 dial 26 countries. We are within sight of the day when any subscriber in the world will be able to dial any other.

Television also is making increasing use of satellites. Major events in our country increasingly are being shown live over large areas of the world. Some hundred of millions of viewers watch the annual Eurovision song contest. There are 80 million television sets in Western Europe alone. There is also a considerable inter-change of broadcasting material between countries. The Cherokee and the Sioux have invaded half the world and family life has stood still across the globe while the Forsytes went their intriguing ways.

The development of jet travel and telecommunications are indeed contracting the world but another recent event has reduced us still further. 'A small step for man but a giant leap for mankind', said Neil Armstrong as he stepped down on to the surface of the moon. Man had crossed the threshold of inter-stellar travel and in so doing had reduced the dimensions of his world to an orange hanging above the horizon. The first space ships to orbit Mars were launched in the summer of 1971. There can be little doubt that the techniques of space travel will be developed to carry man to the planets before the end of this century maybe to colonise, maybe to exploit mineral deposits, when the infant-school child of today has children of his own in the infant school.

The contraction of the world by improved communication and travel will go on. The advance of technology is cumulative. The graph is not a straight line but a steeply curved one. The progression is geometrical not arithmetical. Because of this, we are not preparing our children to live in today's smaller world but in the nutshell world of A.D. 2000 onwards and the consequences of this for education are enormous. They demand nothing less than a new orientation of educational philosophy, rooted as it is at present in the attitudes, outlooks, prejudices and myths of national sovereignty, to guide education in an age when the sovereign state will be an irrelevance. Education is in the main provided by the state and is expected to play a major part in preserving national identity, to a lesser extent in the schools of an old and mature country like Britain than in the U.S.A., with its daily nationalistic ritual. It has traditionally an obligation to contribute to the unity and separateness of the state which provides it but the contraction of the world is rapidly creating a more important obligation to the unity and indivisibility of mankind. Until it is accepted as the more important both by those engaged directly in education and by their paymasters, there will be increasing tension between the two, almost the basic individual v. society educational dilemma discussed in Chapter 1 on a global, nation v. mankind scale. And the tension will call for considerable courage from educationists in the face of chauvinistic pressure not to raise their sights beyond the national boundary in spite of our shrinking world. But the pressure must be withstood for today's children will, in adult life, regard themselves more as citizens of the world than their parents do today. The quality of their lives will depend to a considerable extent on whether or not they can do so without strain, without conflict—or whether they will carry national outlooks, inhibitions and prejudices into a world which is too small for them.

By far the most important and urgent problems are those created by the deep and ancient prejudices which are evoked by colour and race: important because they are immoral; urgent because as the world contracts the danger from this prejudice escalates from the bow-and-arrow level to the H-Bomb level. The smaller the world, the greater the danger.

Although it is one of mankind's most universal and intractable problems it is remarkable how little is known about its causes. No doubt it stemmed originally from fear of the unknown, the unfamiliar, the black face, the strange language, the 'heathen' rites; but it has now become woven into social attitudes and social behaviour, handed on from one generation to another.

But we do not really know why, without apparent reason, strong, often violent, feelings are aroused by the presence of people of another race living among us. Clearly it is unreasonable, illogical, immoral, un-Christian to have hatred or dislike for someone because his race, colour, creed or customs are different from our own—but this prejudice exists among large numbers of people even in a country of liberal traditions like Britain and much more so in a country like South Africa where state policy is actually motivated by it.

Since the dismantling of the nineteenth-century empires, there has been considerable movement among the former colonial peoples, usually towards the old imperial country. In our own case it has been made easier until recently because of the concept of a common strand of citizenship. Imperialism occasionally had an enlightened idea! In 1966 there were 853,000 new commonwealth immigrants in Great Britain. Between 1961 and 1966 the number increased by 9·5 per cent annually. This was the period of most rapid entry. The rate of increase has fallen since then but the number of immigrant children in the schools has increased from 131,000 in 1966 to about 250,000 in 1969. These are distributed in 10,000 schools out of our total of 30,000. Thus about a third of our schools are now multi-racial. Distribution varies enormously and surprisingly, e.g. Bolton has 1,900 immigrant pupils and Wigan 19. The Runnymede Trust, by making the most generous assumptions, has calculated that by 1985 the coloured population of Britain will be slightly under three millions.

The immigrant population has given education in Britain an opportunity to make a contribution to the world-wide problem of combating race and colour prejudice—and it cannot be eliminated by legislation. The Law may punish positive racial discrimination as, to our credit, it now does in Britain, but it can never pluck the cause of the discrimination from the mind of the discriminator. Education can probably begin to do so but only if this becomes a major educational objective.

Chapter 5 was a plea not only for education to revive and sustain democracy but also to apply it in its content, method and organisation by a recognition of the equal importance of each individual child—and this includes black and brown as well as white. Chapter 4 reached the conclusion that in moral and religious teaching respect for the personality and the search for truth are the most important elements—and, indeed, they are the two Great Commandments. Chapter 3 put the view that the only basis for authority in the modern world is the involvement and consent of the individual. Even Chapter 2 in its forecast of the demands on education of the age of technology saw a re-birth of man the individual in place of man the cog. Wherever one turns societal change, even technological change, demands a reinstatement of the dignity and supreme importance of the individual person after two centuries of industry-induced uniformity, the rise of empires and all the exploitation of coloured people which followed and their subsequent fall, the rise of the authoritarian regimes with the fall of some and the evolution of others.

Surely, the contraction of the world points the same direction for education. We are all part of a human family being thrown closer together by the increase in our numbers and the growth of our technology. Self-interest as well as common humanity demands that education everywhere should wage an unrelenting war on the ancient prejudices of colour and race. And British education has at the moment an opportunity to make a significant contribution to this major, worldwide need. This is the starting point of any review of the so-called 'immigrant problem' in our schools. It gives us a chance we have never had before in Britain, except in some of our more enlightened imperial moments, to help to bridge the unreasoning, hateful gulfs between Asian, African and European. It is an opportunity to do the job that education is about—establishing the identity and equal importance of all human beings.

There is another way in which the presence of Asian and West Indian children in our schools is a clear gain. Their different cultural backgrounds can, if used sensitively, considerably enrich the life of the schools and the cultural development of both pupils and teachers. The Pakistani child must be encouraged to take pride in his own culture even though he is acquiring a new one—but how often does he come to look upon it as second-rate and almost unmentionable, an impediment which is best forgotten in a world of western values. This arrogant assumption of western superiority which allows, indeed encourages, the obliteration of other cultures which could enrich our own is the fertile source of much race prejudice. There should be an acceptance of diversity and not an attempt to create homogeneity. We should keep both the Sikh turban and the Welsh language.

Religion is one aspect of culture where there is considerable opportunity for cross-fertilisation. It is important for Christian children to know that there are more followers of Islam in the world than there are Christians and to know about and understand the large area of common ground between the two. Religious education and the morning assembly should establish this common ground. And will the Almighty mind very much whether we call him God or Allah?

Let us then begin by seeing both the opportunity and the enrichment our immigrants bring to British schools and stop regarding them as a burden to be dispersed, forgotten or absorbed.

Secondly they must be accorded complete equality of educational opportunity to develop their potential with the indigenous child population. Mr. H. E. R. Townsend, Senior Research Officer to the N.F.E.R., in an address on 1 December 1970, said that 43 of the 70 local educational authorities with immigrants had secondary selection. Less than half kept records of separate immigrant selection but these showed that overall transfer to selective schools was 18–30 per cent but for immigrants 0–5 per cent. This is very far from equality of opportunity and indicates that the educational disadvantage of our immigrant children is as bad as that of our own lower working class. Philip Mason has pointed out in *Patterns of Dominance* (Oxford University Press, 1970) that '... whatever injustice or imperfection exists within a society will be brought to light by the presence of a group thought of as different.'

But equality of educational opportunity does not mean that immigrant children will respond to the same teaching in the same way as British-born children. This has become obvious even in the basic educational task of learning English. Schools are still to be found where 14-year-old Indian boys are learning to read on a diet of Janet and John! However, in recent years it is being done a good deal more effectively. We have progressed from the Ministry of Education 1963 pamphlet: *English for Immigrants* which was based on what J. H. Mundy described in *Trends in Education* (October 1970) as the 'osmosis' theory of language teaching—picking it up in the classroom—to the Schools Council Working Paper, No. 31. *Immigrant Children in Infant Schools* which advocates a more systematic and controlled approach.

Some local authorities are going to great lengths to disseminate information about teaching methods. The Department for the Teaching of English as a Second Language at Birmingham with a staff of 40 peripatetic teachers is an excellent example of enlightened local-authority initiative in this field, although on the whole there has been remarkably little pooling of experience between either schools or local authorities. Few of the 70 local education authorities with immigrants have a local inspector or organiser wholly assigned to immigrant education although about 70 combine this responsibility with remedial work generally.

The problem of finding appropriate teaching methods is complicated by a good deal of recent research which shows that different ethnic groups have significantly different *patterns* of ability. This has emerged from the work of Lesser, Fife and Clark in the U.S.A. where a variety of tests were given to Chinese, Negro, Jewish and Puerto Rican children. Professor P. Vernon has found similar differences in patterns among Jamaican, Indian, African and Eskimo children. It is probable that the differences are due to cultural and

K

economic background rather than to genetic factors but, whatever the origin, the evidence that they exist is now too well established to be ignored. This research and its important consequences for the teacher in the immigrant schools were discussed by Dr. Stephen Wiseman in the lecture referred to on page 80.

Professor A. R. Jensen, in his controversial paper in the *Harvard Educational Review* (June, 1969) claimed that his investigations among Caucasians and Negroes in the U.S.A. showed that there are genetic differences between the distribution of the measured intelligence of these two groups. These findings are not by any means conclusive but if they were race prejudice would still be immoral and the educational objective of eliminating it would still be no less important and urgent.

If such basic abilities as verbal ability, reasoning, number facility, etc., vary according to the ethnic groups to produce differing *patterns* of ability in Asian, European, and African children the teacher's approach must vary from one group to another both to develop aptitudes and to compensate for deficiencies. Here again, as throughout the whole field of present-day educational practice all children must be treated as individuals, each one as a special case.

Thirdly, although it goes without saying that in the organisation and practice of the school no whiff of intolerance or discrimination should be tolerated, a great deal more positive teaching is necessary to normalise relations between ethnic groups and expose the unreason and immorality of many adult attitudes. The positive encouragement of good race relations must now be accepted as a major educational objective.

This will partly be pursued in the context of moral education and its exploration of real-life situations which, in many of our communities today would include an element of race. Where significant race prejudice exists however, it may be counter-productive to attack it frontally. The more fruitful approach would probably be to begin by encouraging attitudes of compassion and tolerance generally and when these are firmly established to apply them to situations involving race. The important point is that race relations should be part of human relations generally and not regarded as *sui generis.*

A good deal of help to teachers is available from the Schools Council Moral Education Project which started work in 1967 with Mr. Peter McPhail as director. Like the approach of the Farmington Trust referred to in Chapter 4, it accepts that morality today is largely autonomous, that moral education must be concerned with the need for a caring relationship with other people and with helping young people to work out their own attitudes and decisions in the light of this relationship and after thinking through the consequences of possible decisions. It is concerned with moral *education,* i.e. encouraging moral behaviour, and not moral *training.*

The Project's programme progresses from simple everyday social situations to more complex topics involving scope for discussion, drama, creative writing, art, research, etc. A number at each stage include race. Apart from the later material which deals with recent problems in the world the situation material dealing with race has been tested in schools. This has ensured the relevance and validity of the material but it has also brought to light the fact that a programme of this kind is just as necessary in the schools where there is no immigrant population as it is in Birmingham and Wolverhampton. Race prejudice is unfortunately universal. A word of caution is necessary. It is important that moral education projects and discussions should not become obsessive about race. It is possible to create problems where none exist and there are the feelings of immigrant children themselves to be considered.

Finally, parental attitudes are of particular importance in immigrant education. So often the Indian girl in the gym-slip returns to another culture of values, language, customs, dress and food when she goes home. In the interests of the child there is everything to be said for positive action by the school to contact the home and to bring the parents into the school. In progressive schools there is also a need to explain their methods to Asian parents whose ideas of education are still based on the Victorian army schoolmaster of the British Raj. Some schools run afternoon classes for Asian mothers. This is excellent—provided father is not forgotten for he is usually the dominant figure in the home.

Thus the immigrant child brings to British schools his opportunities and his problems. The problems are insoluble unless we also recognise and seize the opportunities. They are equally insoluble if the objective is to preserve the pre-immigrant character of our schools with dispersal policies and the like. Many of them are now multi-racial schools and the sooner we accept this fact the better. The problems of the immigrant child require an understanding of *his* educational needs and he, in a democracy—and one which still refers to itself as Christian—has as much right as anyone else to have his education based on his needs and not on someone else's needs, or on what someone else thinks his needs ought to be. Here is the teacher's greatest chance to respond to the shrinking world's demands on education.

But there are other consequences for education. Its content must begin to reflect the world environment more than the national one. Of course love of one's country is deep, old, important, and, on the whole, creditable. Many psychological studies have been made into attachment to and nostalgia for familiar places. They probably derive not from the place but from our links with people associated with them. But they can, and often do, degenerate into silly and even harmful jingoism. We all have many loyalties and one of the purposes of education should be to enable us to arrange them into a coherent pattern with the conflicts resolved—love for, and interest in, one's own part of the earth's surface and its people but in a context of love for mankind and an interest in human beings, their development and doings, everywhere.

Kenneth Clark became a household name in the spring of 1969 because of his series of television programmes on Civilisation. The breadth of his survey is seen from the 238 illustrations in the published scripts which range from the prow of a viking ship to a Karsh picture of Einstein (*Civilisation*, B.B.C. & John Murray, 1969). The notice on the cover describes it as 'A personal view of how Western Europe evolved after the collapse of the Roman Empire and produced the ideas, books, buildings, works of art and great individuals that make up a civilisation.' And this could well be the theme of a course of study which should find its place in all our schools. Like civilisation itself it would not be fragmented into subjects or end at the English Channel. It would include art, design, literature, music, architecture, ideas, religions, societies and their organisations from the family to the United Nations and beyond, science and mathematics, history and its inter-relationship with geography—all unfolding the forward march of mankind, all opening outwards from the child himself to the world and the civilisation which nurtures him, from the present to all the past and the future. Can't we now get away from the 'boxes of knowledge' type of curriculum and examination syllabus? (National boxes of knowledge at that!)

One aspect of the world-wide canvas on which the modern curriculum must be painted will be of considerable importance in the sheer mechanics of living in the smaller world—the mastery of languages other than one's own. Of course there is more to languages than the mechanics of international living. They are a major element in national culture and ought to be studied in their cultural and human context so that mastery of them increases understanding beyond an enhanced power to communicate.

In 1964 the government initiated a pilot scheme of teaching French in primary schools. The N.F.E.R. is now surveying the results. A second interim report covering the transition of 12,000 children from primary to secondary school was published in December 1970 (*French in the Primary School: Attitudes and Achievements*). The survey so far, if more widely disseminated, could improve language teaching generally. In particular it underlines the close connection between fluency and teacher (including headteacher) enthusiasm. There is also further evidence, if any were needed, of the influence of home background on achievement, an aspect which is also currently being investigated in a project financed by the Department of Education and Science at Birkbeck College, University of London. Not the least important part of the survey was concerned with the attitudes of the pupils themselves. Many thought the material was too contrived and unrelated to real-life situations. Not unnaturally those who had been to France made most progress and got the greatest enjoyment out of it.

This experiment has demonstrated the feasibility and advantage of teaching another language in the primary school but it has operated to the detriment of other languages in the secondary school. The children who had already spent three years learning French obviously had to continue with it instead of being able to begin German or some other language. This has also created problems for the schools themselves.

But, one wonders, why the near-monopoly of French continues—particularly as there is a shortage of teachers of French. In A.D. 2000 the major world languages will almost certainly be English, Russian and Chinese. France is our nearest neighbour and we have our sentimental, nineteenth-century attachment to its language. But today's children who will move about the world a great deal and pick up sufficient French to get by anyhow, are much more likely to want to speak to the people of these two vast nations whose regimes will inevitably become more liberal and less introverted. They also have to live in the contracting world.

The Nuffield/Schools Council Russian Course found that, provided the material is well planned and attractive, Russian could be introduced with success at 11. But why not a primary-school Russian Experiment?—or, if the teachers can be found, a Chinese experiment? A widespread expansion of the teaching of these two languages is clearly essential on any estimate of the needs of the world when our children will be middle-aged. But a start must be made now by the universities and colleges of education increasing the number and capacity of courses for teachers—

'There is a ridiculous bottleneck for would-be-linguists at university level: there are insufficient places for all the good candidates who apply. . . .' (Brian Ellis in *Trends in Education*, October 1970.)

Mankind, unfortunately, is stuck with the Tower of Babel but at least we should begin to ensure that a majority of us understand each other.

Allied with language learning but also as part of the world-wide curriculum much greater efforts must be made to facilitate international educational exchanges of pupils and students. Could we not now begin to aim at a full term spent in another country for all pupils in their statutory school life? It should not be beyond us to make reciprocal arrangements with other countries, again not limited to Western Europe but going to countries further afield including Canada and the U.S.A. Some schools are already taking imaginative and valuable initiatives in this direction, e.g. the Dartington Hall School voluntary service project in Sicily.

Short of exchanges and periods spent abroad a great deal more could be done to establish close links with schools in other lands, e.g. a rural school in Britain, given the equipment and enthusiasm, could establish intimate and close relations with a prairie school in Canada by short-wave ratio, or a school in London with one in New York or Sydney. The barriers of distance no longer exist and we must stop pretending that they do.

Finally, we are more aware than ever before of world problems and major problems throughout the world. We see the Vietnam War on our television screens day after day. When the Korean War started Mr. Attlee, then Prime Minister, said it was a conflagration which could burn our own house down. But they are so familiar that it is easy not to take an interest in them. Yet world citizenship, as well as the caring attitude which this book has advocated, demands that we should regard them as our problems—not someone else's, e.g. such great issues as world poverty and illiteracy, the survival of parliamentary democracy in Asia, apartheid, race in the U.S.A., the control of nuclear weapons, European integration, ought to find their place in the curriculum, not only because they will profoundly affect tomorrow's world but also because they often raise issues which moral education cannot ignore.

Chapter 7 discussed the diminishing cohesion of the social groups in which we live our lives and the consequent problems of personal security and identity. As the concept of the homogeneous national group is eroded by the pressure of the contracting world similar problems—but writ larger—will emerge. Education by a

wider vision, by involvement in mankind and its problems everywhere must enable the next generation to feel secure and preserve
their identity when the world is their village—

'I love Britain. But to suggest to a student that he might dedi-
cate his life to the erasure of pollution, or the restoration of the
environment too closely resembles cabin painting as the ship
sinks to really challenge. We will only give our lives to something
that is fast enough and free enough to use all our energies for the
rest of our lives. We could not be satisfied to stop at the recon-
struction of Britain, or the unification of Europe; anything that
will not set out to house, clothe and feed all men in dignity and
fill empty hands with work, and empty hearts with a satisfying
idea, is too small for us.' (Extract from a letter to *The Times*, 3rd
May 1971, by Mr. G. L. McAll, a student at Magdalene College,
Cambridge.)*

* Quoted by permission of *The Times* and of Mr. McAll.

10

Conclusion

A number of aspects of contemporary society have been considered in the foregoing chapters together with the responses which they appear to demand from education. Running through them all, indeed wherever one looks in the modern world, is the common factor of the supreme importance of the individual child and his need for an education which by its organisation, content and method will unfold and preserve his uniqueness, and, which is longer in time, broader in scope and greater in relevance to his life and problems than it is at present for very many of our children. This is the opposite of an education aimed at the norm with which we have had to make do for so long. Education systems, curricula or teaching methods designed for the norm are, by definition, inappropriate for the large majority.

The gathering momentum of technology calls for those individual qualities which have not been in great demand in the machine age of the past two centuries with its production-line outlook—flexibility, creativity, all-round understanding, compassion but also objectivity —all qualities requiring a longer, broader, more individualised education. Paradoxically, the exploitation of the machine which has reached its present point by narrower and narrower specialisms can only be carried further by broadening the base of education.

New attitudes to authority are a dominating and worrying fact of life to most teachers today. They will not change or go away by being ignored. They are the product of a century of change but if their permanence is accepted and new approaches to 'order' worked out in the classroom and on the campus the result will be wholly beneficial to pupil, teacher and society. They are certainly a challenge but they are also an opportunity to create relations which will be more productive of good in education than we have ever known.

The only worthwhile kind of authority the teacher can possess today is that which—like the authority of the Great Teacher—is based on free acceptance and not on status, law, a code or fear. The condition-precedent for this is that the dignity, integrity and importance of each child must be respected and that all children, able and less able, working class and middle class, catholic and protestant, coloured and white, down-town and lush suburb, are esteemed equally. And all this has implicit in it an end to authoritarian school and college regimes and teaching methods.

The waning of Christian commitment, the consequent widespread refusal to regard Christianity as the only worthwhile source of morality and the growth of autonomous morality also elevate the individual child to the very centre of the school's efforts to teach morality, for if standards of morality are to be decided by each individual by his own reason and in his own heart every child must be a special case demanding the individual help of his teachers.

The growing disenchantment with democracy, its remoteness and its apparent sluggish inefficiency can only be dispelled if each child learns to think for himself, to have the ability and courage to face all the facts about his problems and to use his judgment on them to reach balanced conclusions. But there must also be practice in democracy in the schools and colleges as well as in its decision-making techniques—and there is precious little democracy in some of our educational institutions where harsh authoritarian regimes and teaching methods live on.

Above all perhaps, all who are involved in educational provision from the minister allocating resources to the headteacher deploying his teachers, equipment and teaching space must change the deeply-rooted attitude which believes it right to divert more resources and the best resources where they are least needed.

If the starting point of democracy is that all members of society are of equal importance we must by better teaching methods, by socially just organisational patterns both within school and in the localities, remove those gross inequities which deface education in this country and deny equality of opportunity to vast numbers of children. Little wonder our democracy is viewed with such utter cynicism when we consider some of the features of our education system. Yet the health and vitality of a democracy are highly relevant to the quality of life in it. And that is what education is about.

The now clearly established relationship between measured ability and social class, the massive educational disadvantage suffered by the children of working-class families and our continuing failure to make compensatory education a first priority as well as all the continuing practices such as ability streaming which are based on measured ability which is, in fact, significantly a measure of social background, are central defects in British education. Here again, our new knowledge about intelligence and its relation to social class points clearly to the importance of treating each child and his circumstances as a special case as well as to the urgent need for longer formal education for children who will only get it if it is statutorily enforced.

The loosening bonds of community life, in particular in the family, creating almost widespread social deprivation among children, also place firmly upon the school a further duty to compensate by improving the quality of its corporate life and by encouraging a sense of communal responsibility. Both require that children shall be treated as individuals each one of whom is in need of affection, security and approbation, but each one's needs will be different in some respects from those of others—sometimes marginally, sometimes massively. They are needs which cannot be met in the mass. Every child in every group has a different pattern of social need and a different set of personal relations within the group. He is, in this as in everything else, a very special case.

Similarly, the teacher's inescapable obligation to be concerned with the use of leisure in the twenty-first century can only be discharged by nurturing personal growth and all those qualities such as lively-mindedness, flexibility, creativity and compassion which flow from an individual approach to his children and to their needs as they see them.

The ability to communicate is a great deal more than mechanical skills in speech, writing or the deciphering of written symbols which may be acquired from mass instruction. It also involves the transmission to others of the individual's knowledge, ideas and feelings. It is a vehicle for the assertion of individual uniqueness—for all the riches which can flow from the mind, heart and soul of a person who has become truly himself, the means by which his distinctive strand can be woven into the common pattern. If the growth of our many-sided humanity is to be the objective the power to communicate is an essential corollary. Without it there is nothing. With it all the shining glories of a new being can be possessed vicariously by his fellows. Whether the communication be by spoken word, written symbol, drama, painting, sculpture, music, ballet or by any other skill, it always serves the creation of personal identity and education is about the creation of identity.

The contracting world will bring increasing pressures—problems of race, language, economics and politics which will require skills as well as adaptability, forbearance and understanding of an order previously unknown. These qualities are not the end-products of the production-line type of education. They can only be developed in a teaching situation which values and applies them itself. If our children are to retain their freedom and identity in the hazel-nut world of the next century they must emerge from our education system informed, unprejudiced, courageous and compassionate individuals able to think for themselves, unafraid of change and innovation, able to appreciate the other man's problem and share his burdens.

Thus, wherever we look in the strange, brave new world in which our children will live their adult lives the same educational objectives emerge. They are the nurturing of the uniqueness of each child with all the undoubted risks involved, a wider curriculum which respects the oneness of knowledge and is dictated more by the child's self-assessed needs than by adult assessment of them and the development of reason and objectivity but both tempered by compassion.

Broad objectives of this kind have a number of practical consequences. Our statutory school life must be extended at both ends to cater for the precious years of early infancy and for the tumultuous years of late adolescence. Universal provision of nursery education is surely a first priority—particularly if social disadvantage is ever to be neutralised. At the other end the aim should be a leaving age of 18 for all, poor as well as rich, by the end of the present decade. These are costly educational advances but we dare not, and ought not to, afford not to make them.

Central to educational provision as well as to the philosophy of this book must be a massive national effort to reduce the size of teaching groups so that our teachers can teach individuals. In 1971 we have a national pupil-teacher ratio of 22·6 but we also have over 6 per cent of our classes with over 40 pupils. Little wonder many of our teachers cannot, with the best will in the world, break away from the old class-teaching techniques of the past.

But teaching-group size is the product of two factors—teacher supply and the availability of buildings. Clearly a sustained national effort is required if we are ever to enable the schools to improve the relevance of the education they provide. Not to make this effort both to provide the teachers and the buildings will be extremely wasteful for our teachers will be forced to teach for an age which has gone—an age in which the individual mattered less.

There must clearly be an end to the closing of educational options at the age of 11—or at any other age. Our knowledge about the social factor in measured ability has reduced 11 + selection to an educational obscenity which must be ended before we can begin to claim any democracy in our education system.

Similarly, our new knowledge about the deleterious effects of ability streaming demand an end to this demoralising, soul-destroying practice. How dare we continue to coach for failure in life as well as at school as we do at present in so many schools?

The need for individual growth requires new classroom systems of programmed learning to enable each child to progress at his own speed. Educational technology must be regarded as the concern of every teacher. It requires more resources and a more effective dissemination of its data and products.

New links are needed between local social service departments and the schools to enable early detection of children in distress of whom there are probably well over 100,000 in our schools. In addition, more colleges of education could follow the lead of Ede Hill College, Liverpool, in providing training in social work for teachers. Social detriment which depresses school performance must be diagnosed and appropriate compensatory action taken if this large submerged group of our children are to have a reasonable chance to develop their potential.

Finally, there must surely be an end to our divisive, tripartite system of higher education. In a decade which is faced with the daunting task of doubling the number of places in higher education with all the rationalising of structure which this must entail an opportunity presents itself to re-model the system on more democratic lines which reflect the changes taking place in the secondary schools. What is quite certain is that by the end of the decade we shall hear with increasing insistence the demand for tertiary education for all. Let us hope that it will be met more speedily than Tawney's call for secondary education for all in the 1920's!

Of course this amounts to a thorough-going, top-to-bottom democratisation of education—its philosophy, values, systems, practices, methods and content. Nothing less will meet the challenge of tomorrow—and it is in tomorrow's world that our children will live and work.

Our teachers and all engaged in education have a duty to take, from time to time, a long cool look at the society which employs them, to criticise if need be, not necessarily to follow slavishly every whim of fashion, but always to make their practice relevant to it and its needs. Formal education probably cannot fundamentally change a free society. There are too many other educational influences—particularly the mass media and the home. It can and should try to influence trends in it—sometimes to counteract, sometimes to divert, sometimes to accelerate but never to ignore.